A Kite of Farewells

O. Jungio is an assistant research officer for the Department of Arts & Culture, Government of Nagaland. When he is not writing, you can find him noodling on the guitar and the ukulele or cooking up kooky projects for his YouTube channel (an interesting project of late is 'Screaming Plant', a device that allows a plant to 'scream' when it's 'thirsty'). He can be reached at ovungjungio8@gmail.com.

'Ovung masterfully holds the reader's attention with gripping stories that evoke glimpses of the contemporary Naga life—a fast-changing world where an acute sense of nostalgia pervades the everyday and old ghosts lie in wait underneath the façade of modern civilization.'

—Avinuo Kire, author of
The Last Light of Glory Days and Other Stories

A Kite of Farewells
Stories from Nagaland

O. Jungio

Published by
Rupa Publications India Pvt. Ltd 2025
7/16, Ansari Road, Daryaganj
New Delhi 110002

Sales centres:
Bengaluru Chennai
Hyderabad Jaipur Kathmandu
Kolkata Mumbai Prayagraj

Copyright © Ovungthung Jungio 2025

This is a work of fiction. Names, characters, places and incidents are either the product of the author's imagination or are used fictitiously and any resemblance to any actual person, living or dead, events or locales is entirely coincidental.

All rights reserved.

No part of this publication may be reproduced, transmitted, or stored in a retrieval system, in any form or by any means, electronic, mechanical, photocopying, recording or otherwise, without the prior permission of the publisher.

P-ISBN: 978-93-6156-590-8
E-ISBN: 978-93-6156-768-1

First impression 2025

10 9 8 7 6 5 4 3 2 1

The moral right of the author has been asserted.

This book is sold subject to the condition that it shall not, by way of trade or otherwise, be lent, resold, hired out, or otherwise circulated, without the publisher's prior consent, in any form of binding or cover other than that in which it is published.

*To the boy
who never smiled in class group photos.*

> 'Let everything
> Happen to you.
> Beauty and terror.
> Just keep going.
> No feeling is final.'

—RAINER MARIA RILKE

Contents

Preface / xi
Translated Terms / xiii
Fire / 1
Scoreboard / 11
Eyes of the Tiger / 27
The Encyclopaedia Salesman / 38
Showroom / 46
Page 59 / 54
About a Chair / 63
Code Blue / 73
Flower in the Wild / 82
Time / 90
Scared Crow / 108
The Newspaper Kite / 137
Acknowledgements / 146

Preface

IN THE QUIET THEATRE OF memory, where the past takes centre stage, *A Kite of Farewells* is a poignant—and, at times, absurd—anthology of departure. Each story within these pages is tethered to an object that bears silent witness to the lives that once brushed against its form.

As you turn these pages, you will encounter tales that weave the threads of loss, each narrative a delicate strand in the fabric of existence. The objects—mute spectators to human sorrow—become the vessels of collective grief, the repositories of the most intimate of farewells. These stories are like the eponymous kite, soaring high, carrying with it memories and goodbyes, perhaps symbolizing the soul's journey or the act of releasing emotions and memories into the sky.

But these stories are also a celebration of the bonds that outlast mortality. They contain the love that lingers in the grain of a wooden table, the comfort that resides in the well-worn creases of a chair, the voices that echo in the empty spaces of a room.

A Kite of Farewells

This collection invites you to explore the depth of human connections and the artefacts that become the legacy of those connections. It is a testament to the enduring power of memory and the resilience of the human spirit in finding beauty even in the face of absence.

Translated Terms

Alu	Potato
Amo	Uncle
Amotsu	Grandfather
Ango	Younger brother/son
Ano	Aunty
Apo	Father
Ata	Elder brother/sister
Atsu	Grandmother
Ayo	Mother
Biri	Cigarette
Chulha	A firewood-based stove
Echu Li	Part of Lotha folklore, a place where the dead go before they pass on to the final resting place, a purgatory of sorts
Gaon bura	A village elder man appointed by the government, usually with in-depth knowledge about the local customs and practices
Gutka	Chewing tobacco
Jaha	Tea

A Kite of Farewells

Joka	Kitchen
Kaka	Sister
Kata biskot	Local rusk biscuit
Magur	Catfish
Majhung	A verandah raised on a platform
Moora	Sitting stool
Morung	A bachelor dormitory that used to be a centre for learning during pre-colonial times
Motu ghors	Dingy local pubs
Nimotsu	Your grandfather
Ngongo	Son
Okharo	Youngest son
Raja machi	King chilly
Wai Wai	A popular instant-noodles brand
Zutsu	Rice beer

Fire

*I*T WAS ONLY AFTER I had driven a few kilometres away from the town gate that it dawned on me that an object of great interest was missing—Ayo's casserole. She was adamant and convincingly persuasive about staying away from those roadside hotel foods, which, in her words, were vectors for every ungodly disease in the world masquerading as something palatable. Exaggerating with a yelp, she painstakingly narrated in unnerving detail a recent incident of dubious origin about a certain unwary traveller who collapsed into his plate of steaming momos after taking a coy bite.

'It's the dust. And the unhygienic kitchen. And the utensils. And...the people serving it.'

I imagined the look of horror on her face upon the discovery of the casserole lying unmoved on the dining table, but it might have escaped her sight since I had not been inundated with phone calls already. Besides, if there was anything that our house owned in sheer abundance, it was those damned casseroles, and in all honesty, every

A Kite of Farewells

one of them looked near identical—porcelain with a lazy floral pattern aimed at a just-adequate aesthetics. In a house where everyone has their biological clocks chaotically out of sync—it's a wonder we all somehow manage to come together for the evening prayer everyday—Ayo had taken upon herself the paramount duty of putting forth a warm meal for anyone who bothered to darken the kitchen door, notwithstanding the position of the hour hand of the clock.

I wasn't supposed to be on the road at this hour of the day, or even on this day of the week. An impromptu inspection-cum-visit from the headquarters had prompted me to schedule this lone journey on the mud-caked highway that had conspicuous signs of poor workmanship all over it and was looking to be further humiliated by the swelling mass of grey clouds gathering above. For the first hour, I drove past lulling sights of people in varied shapes and shoddy establishments wearing a desperate look of invitation for whatever crumbs of attention the few souls passing through could toss into their direction. I did my fair share of charity by waving at some kids huddled around a sleepy chulha, clad in grimy and soiled second-hand pullovers. They frantically gestured towards me in unison but I couldn't make out if it was juvenile mischief or plain old courtesy.

It started to drizzle by the time I made it past the last house on the stretch. For something so impoverished in appearance, the sight of the flowers in full bloom the colour of sapphire against the freshly plastered mud walls of the house lent to it a certain richness that went beyond mere description in impassioned prose.

A few turns around unsuspicious bends, and I found myself driving through a thick blanket of mist and rain—both becoming increasingly indistinguishable from each other with every passing minute—descending relentlessly upon the naked skin of the earth. I reckoned I would be making an unanticipated stop if the rain persisted. Just when I was about to navigate the possibility of that thought, I was greeted with an unceremonious vista of a cranky queue snaking up to an occupied crane that was heaving off a mass of sludgy rocks splayed over the road ahead. My stomach protested by releasing loud groans from its pit.

I got out of the car, dragged myself through the slushy road to survey the situation up ahead. The crane operator, a man not inclined towards stray conversation, muttered that it would take longer than usual to clear the way. What the usual was in a conundrum like this was beyond my limited reasoning. Upon my persistent enquiry, he muttered again, this time clearly annoyed, that I should go grab something to eat because it might go on till the night. The man obviously spoke from experience, so I obliged.

The only problem now was to find a respectable establishment nearby to idle around—there was nothing there other than trees and dust.

A pimply faced guy hunched over the steering wheel just two vehicles behind mine was kind enough to impart his knowledge of the area by mentioning some village around

A Kite of Farewells

a certain corner to the right. In that brief conversation, my attention was expended on mapping the rugged contours of his face—an unnecessary but unavoidable distraction.

Through the hazy blanket of mist, the sun had shrunk into a pale orange imitation of its boisterous self. Suddenly, the certainty of a long, cold October night without a sturdy roof above my head to await the dawn seemed like a vague possibility. And I, in more animated parlance, was starving like a rat in an abandoned mall.

I remembered driving past far too many right turns, only to alight from the vehicle to the mocking sight of yet another fork in the road. For the desire—or need—of a better option, I steered my vehicle to the left this time—and behold! A village gate stuck out through the never-ending foliage. My body was shaken to elation at the discovery. The night belonged to the lesser god of left turns.

When my excitement waned, something odd struck me about the ceremonial village tree adjacent to the entrance gate: it was charred to its last living cell. The imposing, spidery silhouette of its branches, cradling the waft of thick mist around it, played sinister tricks on the eyes.

My attention moved to a heavy set of footsteps accompanied by the jingle-jangle of some metallic antique some distance away. They turned out to belong to a jovial-looking man wearing the longest shawl I had ever seen on a person; its fringes scraped and swept the ground below as he closed the distance between us. In his hand he carried a cranky kerosene lamp; it was unlit and appeared to be so for as long as it had existed. Not wanting to be the harbinger of obvious news, I chose to ignore it for the conversation that was to follow.

'I am keeping guard as the whole village is away for the Great Harvest.'

I was taken aback not only by the nonchalance with which the information was conveyed to me but by the timing—it was too late by any standards to be busying oneself with the toils of farm work.

'They are in the fields at this time of the—' I was cut short before I could complete my question.

'You must be tired. Come with me,' the man spoke to me with such great urgency that it made me follow him without another word wasted on more questions.

We raced through the village gate, and the dingy houses propped up against the blackness of the night, until we came upon the lone guest house in the village.

'This is it,' the man swung the tin door of the village guest house with force. A single dim bulb threw its uneasy swell of orange glow onto the sparse furniture pushed against one side of the wall.

'There is a well behind the house. You can wash up there and come down to the community hall. Food will be ready.'

I couldn't be more elated to hear him mention food—so much so that I curtailed my washing routine to a brisk splashing of cold water on my feet and face, in that particular order.

A Kite of Farewells

After this, I gladly made my way down to the community kitchen, two houses away from the guest house, and proceeded to survey the offering on the table—a stainless steel plate and three clay pots. Without skipping a beat, I reached for the plate and then one of the clay pots but—

The three pots were filled with raw rice, unwashed vegetables and raw pork.

I called out to the man to check if he was around. Upon receiving no answer, I went around for the next twenty minutes from one empty house to another, looking for signs of him. I had every right to be slightly unnerved, but the growing hunger pangs left no room for any other feeling.

I still persisted with the search until it dawned on me that I could very well cook the food myself. Perhaps by way of some idiosyncratic tradition, this village served raw food on this particular day of the Great Harvest, I reckoned.

After fumbling through the first few tries, I managed to get a fire kindling under the clay pot filled with rice and water. A wispy trail of smoke snaked through the chimney, out towards the clear, open sky. Emboldened by the favourable outcome, I also managed to get a bonfire started outside with a few twigs scattered around the premise. The overbearing warmth of it elicited a strange feeling of assurance regarding the night and the journey beyond. Without questioning its salubrious crackle, I dissolved my being into a sleeping puddle of pure contentment on a plastic chair facing the bonfire.

But I was violently shaken out of my short sleep by

Fire

the heavy panting of a man behind me. It was the fellow from earlier, and by the angled furrows in his face, I could tell he was peeved.

'You shouldn't have started a fire in this village!' he shouted at me.

'Why not? You left me with raw rice!' I protested.

'They will surely not forgive you now.'

'They who?' I asked.

'Come, I'll show you.'

We quickly raced towards the village citadel commanding a panoramic view of the area around, right down to the perennial river cutting through the hillocks.

'Them.' He pointed towards the bend leading into the second village gate.

A person with most despicable features pushed into the view, followed by another, and another, until they were a crowd—every one of them looked burnt, with putrid mass of pale flesh hanging off their bodies. Their gaze were locked on me, staring into the deepest recesses of my being and freezing me on the very ground I stood.

'Skin the visitor! Skin the visitor!'

They all shouted in morbid unison as they stomped the ground.

I felt like a helpless bird caught in the eye of a storm.

'What…should I do?'

I turned to the man who for some reason seemed unfazed at the sight beholding us.

'Run. Don't look back. Run for your life,' he said.

A Kite of Farewells

He then broke out into bouts of hysterical laughter, the kind that hung in the air piercing the senses with primal fear. I leaped into a flight for survival.

I ran, tripped and crawled for the longest minutes of my life, until I vanished into the fortified embrace of the metal frame of my vehicle. With my stone-heavy foot against the pedal, I steered it towards the open road, refusing to pay any heed to the unholy commotion on my heels. Within no time, I found myself at the bend offering me a last view of the village gate behind me.

The view that greeted me now was that of the village tree burning with fury. Through the flames, it loomed like an inescapable premonition of a terrible curse.

I drove away till there was nothing but the velvet blur of the night in the rear-view mirror, but the maddening, spine-chilling laughter of that man had managed to race ahead, greeting me at every turn. A part of me echoed its mockery for having expected anything good from strange places and strange people.

My growing concern as the vehicle veered into familiar location was whether the blockade had been cleared.

Thankfully it was, and to serve as a warning, a makeshift 'all good' signpost had been erected near it. The ride on the road gave explicit indication of shoddy workmanship, but at that point I was grateful to have even an inch of open road to get away from what was behind me.

I arrived in the nick of time to one of the roadside hotels pulling down its squeaking shutter. They were kind enough

Fire

to admit a traveller—seemingly shaken out of his civilized demeanour—at such an ungodly hour. It was ten past eight, and the desolate look of the vicinity announced that it was way past Christian bedtime for the locals.

After a hurried meal of omelette and lukewarm coffee, I retired to one of the rooms inside and collapsed into a long night of sleep. In my dream, I faintly remembered a feeling of floating through a valley of voices, guided by the whisper of a woman who eluded my chase in my dream.

I woke up the next day, a little too early, in a pool of sweat.

With the welcome sight of the sun in its ascension warming my petrified soul, I made myself comfortable on one of the three plastic chairs with a plate of hard-boiled eggs and a cup of tea, and made my acquaintance with the early stock of arriving travellers. I managed to strike up a conversation with one headed towards the same road I had arrived from last night. I took my time with the niceties, and when I had him assured of my sanity, I meticulously laid down the ordeal from the previous night. He followed my narration without interruption, perhaps anticipating a crude joke at the end. By the time I finished, his face had assumed a look of animated confusion. What ensued was a long moment of awkward, dead silence.

'If I may say something,' a man sitting beside our table, who had been eavesdropping on our conversation, nudged our exhausted attention to him.

'I heard some of your story, and it brings to my mind an

incident from the '90s about a village that eerily fits your description,' he continued.

'In the early '90s, there was this breakaway village, excommunicated for defiling an ancient artefact, located not far from the blockade area. It was written that before their fated departure, the parent village's headman cursed the exiled lot to be doomed. For some time after its resettlement far from the parent village, it thrived with surplus harvest and a healthy population. But one fated night, while all of them were fast asleep, leaving one man—the village idiot, or so as they called him—who was away in the fields for reasons best known to him, a stray fire in the community hall swelled and enveloped the entire village and its sleeping residents. They say that all of them—men, children, women and beasts—were charred beyond recognition, and upon returning to the village and finding everyone dead, the lone survivor, the village idiot, went full mental.'

The next sip of tea went down my throat like shards of glass against a blackboard.

When the sun finally ushered in the long, sunny day ahead, I got into the vehicle with two tiffin boxes from the hotel, and before I was jerked onwards towards my destination, I could make out from the dust-speckled windshield the man I had earlier made my sorry acquaintance with walking out with the same tiffin boxes—he clearly didn't want to end up hungry in a strange place.

Scoreboard

*N*ZAN ANXIOUSLY PACED UP AND down the corridor of the hospital—lit with lifeless tube lights and wearing an air of unnerving silence. His mother and sister seated outside the operation theatre, fighting sleep and the bitter cold, had been expecting the door of the operation room to swing open any moment for the past four hours. His father had been diagnosed with cancer and this operation was the fourth one so far—a specialist from Delhi had been made available to them after a long waiting period.

'Nzan, come sit here. Everything will be alright,' his mother called.

'When has it ever been alright?' He whispered under his breath as he plopped down on a plastic chair.

◆

It was the summer of 2017 and Nzan had just got back from college after a long, hectic day. He was rummaging through the kitchen for a quick hunger fix as the saucepan on the gas stove rumbled with the frothy sputter of fresh tea.

'Why did I miss lunch?' he sighed.

He flung open every cabinet to hopeless inspection. Finding nothing fancy, he settled on the pot of rice from the morning, which kind of smelt funny. Tucked away in one of the corners behind the stove, he found a small Tupperware with now-forgotten Marie biscuits that had been there for God knows how long. He stuffed the biscuits into his mouth with furious haste. With a pannikin cup filled to the brim with tea, he walked to the back of the kitchen towards the only window looking out into the backyard.

His father, in a faded singlet, was hard at work in the backyard. Beads of sweat trickled down his sun-tanned face as he grinned with satisfaction at the heap of chopped firewood beside him. He would always say that if he could get so much done with a crude eighteenth-century axe, then with an electrical saw they could have a forest to burn by the end of the day.

Nzan sat down on a rattan chair in the verandah and started to skim through *Nagaland Post*. His eyes ran across the headlines that seemed no different from yesterday's and settled on a syndicate-sourced piece about the upcoming FIFA World Cup. As far as his personal history with football—or sports for that matter—went, his participation had been limited to watching his friends make fools of themselves in the annual inter-colony football league year after year. He never understood—or cared enough to understand—why anyone would invest so much into a cup that would be returned

Scoreboard

to the organizer the minute the paltry cash prizes in brown envelopes—it's always brown for some reason—were handed to the top three and the ceremonial photo shoot was over.

'Nzan, come and help me carry these logs to the store room,' his father called out.

Hauling the logs in the folds of his arms, he stacked them in one corner of the store room, and by the time his arms grew weary, that corner had nothing but stacks of logs.

'Apo, *Nagaland Post* has started printing World Cup updates,' he told his father.

'Well, it's time to draw up the scoreboard then.'

'I don't think it will be necessary this time, Apo. You can get match summaries and stats from Google.'

'Well, it has been a tradition for me,' his father said firmly.

The tradition, as his father put it, involved drawing out on a board the predicted match fixtures along with the scores right up to the final showdown. When the prediction didn't hold up to the actual score, he corrected it with a marker. A successful streak of predictions would likely guarantee a reward of cash from the colony lottery pool. The excitement around it whittled down with the advent of dish TV, but back in the days when families used to huddle around the lone cable TV in the whole colony, with their eyes glued to the bulging frame of the small-by-modern-standard CRT TV, the concerted excitement of partaking in a game of prediction and its eventual dismissal or triumph was half the fun of the watching experience, especially with a room full of equally plausible predictions.

A Kite of Farewells

◆

Autumn declared its onset by stripping the grand old tree in the middle of the garden down to its bare branches. Its towering silhouette loomed over the garden fence in the evenings as the dying light of the day blanketed the vegetation in a warm tinge of orange tenderness.

With his dinner—pig fat cooked in bamboo shoots and boiled beans—in one hand and his phone in the other, the evening's quaint offering in the distance was lost on Nzan.

'Nzan, did you find the pig entrails our neighbour gave us this morning?' his mother asked from the kitchen. After a noisy sequence of metallic clangs, and cabinets opening and closing, she came out with a small bowl in her hand.

'Here, have this. You have become so thin.' She emptied the whole bowl onto his plate.

'But Ayo, you like entrails, no?'

'I am cooking magur. It will be done in another ten minutes.'

With dinner done, whatever little remained of the day slipped away like the many days before it, unspectacular and indistinguishable. But up in the hills, there was joy even in the monotony of plain living that the locals themselves wouldn't know how to put into words without sounding a tad bit pretentious.

The next morning, he woke up to the sound of hurried footsteps outside his room. It was six past seven—an hour more and it would be his usual wake-up time. He rubbed the weariness from last night's YouTube binge watch off his eyes and shuffled out, dragging his slippers with commendable effort to fight the early morning inertia. Outside, in the warmth of early sunlight, he saw his sister dashing out from the kitchen. Upon seeing him standing in the verandah and looking like he had great many questions, she called out to him:

'Nzan, you're up? Good. Apo is not feeling well. Can you go up to the junction and wait for the ambulance?'

'Why? What happened?'

'This morning… He vomited blood.'

'Vomited blood?' The news jolted him out of his morning-induced indolence.

For the past two weeks, his father had not been feeling like himself. Truth be told, his condition was worsening by the day. In fact, a week ago he was complaining of intense pain in the stomach, which was shortly followed by intermittent vomiting. Given his father's inclination towards self-medication and weathering sickness till it eventually wanes, it did not surprise anyone that he was popping every pill in the local pharmacy without a prescription.

The events leading from the arrival of the ambulance—surprisingly right on time—to the time his father was helped into the ambulance by the nurses went by in a hazy blur. And by the time he let the event fully register in his mind, his father was laid on the stretcher, helpless, with a confused expression on his face. The ambulance door then shut and it roared off into the distance with his mother and sister inside.

A Kite of Farewells

There is something unsettling about a house when it is left to inactivity all of a sudden. Nzan found himself agitatedly shuttling from one empty room to another for the rest of the day. For once in his life, he found himself facing a strange kind of solitude; it was a feeling of hollow calmness that was slowly ebbing to make way for the approaching storm. When he finally sat down in the sitting room, his eyes settled on a photo album stacked on top of dated *Reader's Digest* issues inside one of the glass cabinets. The album sent him tip-toeing down memory lane. He couldn't help but notice how terribly young his father and mother looked in their early life together as a married couple.

As the evening gave way to the quiet of the night, he pulled out his phone and called his mother for the last time that day. He reckoned network reception must be spotty at the hospital since the call did not connect. He was tired from worrying, and his stomach was putting up a noisy protest over not having eaten anything the whole day. So after a brisk walk in the garden, he came back with some squash that he sliced and dumped into his last-minute substitute dinner: noodles and boiled eggs.

After licking the bowl of noodles clean, he laid down on the bed, his face illuminated by the blue light from the phone screen, on the brink of an all-consuming sleep but also keenly expecting the sound of footsteps outside any time soon.

A thin, dooming voice echoed in the dark recesses of his mind, which made him shift uneasily—bone against flesh. He dared not entertain, especially at this hour, the nihilistic but plausible pronouncement of reason, for it inconvenienced the hope of a better day tomorrow.

◆

'Nzan, your father... The doctor said it's too late,' said his mother on the other end of the phone, on the verge of tearing up. He could make out the faint sobbing of his sister behind his mother.

The revelation didn't quite startle him, but something in the air sharpened his awareness of it; the harsh and bitter truth had now pierced through the veil of foolish optimism.

He cursed his luck, or lack thereof. For Nzan, right at that moment, it felt like fate was slowly twisting her knife of misfortune in his skin.

◆

The pale sky took on a wintery shade as December descended upon the autumn-kissed canopy, blanketing the homely idleness usually characteristic of the desolate and grey winter in this part of the country. Oblivious to the winter settling in, the colony children capered in the local ground, the skinny birds perched on the saggy electric wires overhead continued their noisy gossip, and the chorus of the colony women's choir practice swelled with grandiosity. Those from the hills—born and raised—would eventually get used to the slowness of the dull winter days.

Under at least two mink blankets and wearing the thickest of woollens and polyesters, the people survived December

A Kite of Farewells

nights, and when Christmas decorations came off in January, the coldest month, they would put on another layer.

'There is this bee therapy I read about online. I did not get the time to go through the details, but as far as I understood, it can be *it*—a cure,' said his sister sitting across Nzan at the table. Apo, bent over a bowl of soup, looked pale and bony, direly exhausted even before the day had begun. Nzan nodded to his sister, unsure how to respond. It was not the first time he—and the family—was at the receiving end of his sister's wild theory about potential alternative medicine or miracle cures for cancer that she came across on the kooky side of the Internet. He also remembered an uncle of his who had spoken a week ago of some miracle lemons found in the icy mountains of Tibet that big pharmaceutical companies were hiding from the public. And in spite of the scepticism invited by a claim of such a ludicrous scale, for a dying man hanging on to his dear minutes, the thin line between the absurd and the empirical is blurry; it would also be downright heartless to bring logic into such arguments. Every pinprick of hope is hope nevertheless, even if the respite it offers amounts to nothing more than a fleeting moment of empty faith. Nobody wants to tell a dying man he is going to die, not even the self—especially the self.

◆

Nzan looked at his father who had his head buried in the newspaper with a certain doggedness highlighted in the furrows of his face. The cancer had eroded his body, but his

Scoreboard

mind was busy as ever in pruning and watering the mental landscapes flourishing with daily headlines and whatever was worthy of a debate at the dinner table. Hence, lately the newspaper came to occupy an important place in his daily routine. He read it front to back, slowly and steadily, and when the pages were spent, he would take out a pen or a pencil to busy himself with the daily crossword and Sudoku. For a man who for a large part of his life sweated it out under the sun, it felt odd to witness him in this newfound domesticity.

With January coming to an end, the hospital trips increased in frequency and duration, as did his father's reluctance towards more severe treatments. A week ago, the doctor had suggested chemo to his father, which was met with a sour look of disapproval. Perhaps it was his education—whatever little he had—or his growing distrust in the medical treatment, which frankly had not done much to mitigate his condition. The whispers of ill-informed relatives about the alleged fatality of chemo had only made matters worse. By mid-February, he was in such a sorry shape that he needed assistance with going about his daily routine. Whenever the dreaded talk of going for chemo was brought up by Nzan or some other concerned relative, he would promptly shoot it down. The pronounced effort with which he uttered even the names of people around him made the notion of reasoning with him seem futile—even risky. But some persisted to no avail.

◆

A Kite of Farewells

One evening, as Nzan walked past the common room, he caught a fleeting glimpse of the bare figure of his father bent over the only table in the room, sketching out something with utmost attention. The sharp zipping motion of the marker's tip over the smooth surface of the board, guided by a steel ruler, doused the room with the pitiful frenzy of much-needed activity. Nzan slowly walked up behind Apo and realized that he was drawing up the scoreboard for the World Cup, which of late was becoming the big talk of the town; early enthusiasts in some colonies had already hung up flags of the teams they supported to announce their allegiance. As he leaned in closer, he could make out that Apo's hands were shaking; it seemed like he was skirting on the edge of collapse, like the sputtering old scooter in the garage. But the criss-crossing lines on the board persevered, from one end to another, connecting one block to the next, pitting one team against the other, in a big scheme of even more interconnecting lines until the very top of the board—that empty block that would have the name of the ultimate victor written inside it in all glory. This scoreboard, after it was ready, was to be hung on one of the walls—probably the one behind the TV—and updated as and when each match declared its victor.

That night Nzan dreamt of an erstwhile lover from another small town, but the vagaries of memory that adorned the bitterest of times with profound nostalgia were cut short by the sound of loud sobbing coming from his sister's room. The illuminated edges of her door indicated that lights were still on in her room. It was twenty past midnight and his sister was not usually someone to stay up this late. He wanted to share her grief but decided to let her be, for he himself was not a stranger to such bouts of grief these days, under the blanket of the night's secrecy.

♦

The creeks up the mountains had dried up under the heat of the summer sun. The winding boot prints of hikers were baked on the beaten trails snaking over steep slopes and hair-raising ridges. The woods were alive again, shaken out of the hangover of the winter, and filled with the chirpings of its avian dwellers and the frenzied calls of wild beasts. Every call in the wilderness, away from the maddening monotony of urban life, was an invitation for anyone mad enough to get lost in the hope of finding themselves among the sun-cloaked trees and the tiny echoes of ancient fairies.

Back at home, Nzan was busy on his phone, engrossed in a voiceless conversation with make-believe avatars, sifting through an endless stream of information without much idea about how to dispose of it in a meaningful way, entertaining his primal instincts assured by the offer of anonymity, passing time until the notion of time itself was made absurd in the revelation of the indomitable virus of boredom multiplying in his veins. The fine details of existing are, in all frankness, a boring affair.

'Russia looks promising,' said his father after the debut match between Russia, the host country, and Saudi Arabia

A Kite of Farewells

came to a high-margin end. Russia had managed to net five goals—in a true underdogs-triumph arc—kick-starting the tournament on a surprising note. Nzan looked up from his phone at the TV and then at his father, who was already jotting down the scores on the scoreboard—admonishing his earlier prediction of a lacklustre draw. Usually, he could afford a mistake or two. Just a week ago, he had undergone another operation: his eyes were sunk deep into their sockets and their vacant gaze escaped the light of the sun sometimes.

The usual quiet evenings were now packed with football matches held at the colony's local ground, with some extravagant enough to have jittery sound systems to announce their racket, much to the dismay of the senior citizens, the state competitive exam aspirants, and the chronic naysayers with a local reputation for controversy—mostly the alcoholics. The water-logged football ground—with patches of grass sparingly dotting its expanse, two rusty goal posts sans the net, and a viewing stand littered with packets of gutka and Wai Wai—was seeing an increase in footfall, usually characteristic of a new year's 'variety show' or a visiting out-of-town mela. Two colonies away, a certain someone, as rumours went, painted the wall around his house as the Brazilian flag to complement the table-sized flags hoisted above his roof; stickers of countries and mini-flags were also becoming the most essential car accessories. But ironically, much like a mela, this euphoria was cyclical—the kicking of balls at the local grounds will soon be replaced by swinging of bats, or dribbling of balls, depending on which major sports event was on the TV.

◆

'What's taking them so long? It's already been three hours now.' Nzan craned his neck to look across the corridor again, which wore a look of familiarity now. Even the slightest sound swelled to an echo, rising and crashing like the currents of the Doyang River. Through the slightly open door of one of the many rooms branching from the corridor, he caught a glimpse of a group of nurses in their uniforms huddled in a corner, with their eyes fixed on a football match playing with bare-minimum volume on a conveniently sized TV. It was a knockout match, but the room had as much enthusiasm as a colony Sunday prayer meeting; the nurses' haggard-looking faces and the piercing smell of sterility permeating the hospital elicited collective pity from the people passing through.

The door flung open with a low squeak. Nzan's mother promptly got up from her seat, and the heavy look of exhaustion on her face was taken over with exaggerated restlessness. She peered at the two figures clad in white coats walking out of the room, and far behind them, over their shoulders, into the darkness of the room where all the answers laid, shifting under the unseen currents of vague possibilities. Judging by the solemn look on their faces, she braced herself for the obvious. It was evident to her now that it was only a matter of time. Yet she planted her feet deep into the fertile

A Kite of Farewells

soil of delusional hope. Her prayers and fasting will not—*must not*—be in vain after all. A little more time, *a little more*—not that the heavens will be bankrupted by a little more. Many have asked for more absurd and grander things. Surely God can accommodate her little request.

The doctor ushered the party into his room and sat still, anticipating a question from them. That must have been the longest minute in that corner of the world. Mother, already agitated to desperation, broke the ice by asking the fateful question.

How much time is enough to prepare for the death of a loved one? 'Months,' said the doctor in a whispery tone, as if the tiled walls of his air-conditioned room had conspired to leak every secret spoken within its confines. How much of anything is ever enough for men plagued by the disease of wanting more? Nzan felt that the world would go around just fine if he wanted a little more time for his father. He turned and looked at his mother and sister, their faces more feeble than ever, their pupils dazed under the scrutiny of the harsh ceiling light.

◆

It was a quiet July morning when Apo breathed his last, slipping away into the world of eternal dreams. In the light of the soft morning sun, he laid on the bed, with his thin frame wrapped in a cocoon of blankets: he was finally at peace, away from the clutches of pain. There were tears, lots of them, from neighbours, friends and relatives, each wearing

Scoreboard

a grief as transparent as the other's. A certain frenzy took over the rooms, with people filling every bit of standing and sitting space; the air was thick with the gloom of sorrow. In some corners here and there, whispery conversations could be encountered, peeking and slipping away from the sea of faces.

'Your father is with God now.' Nzan felt his hand go limp as one of his uncles gripped it in a dry handshake. He nodded lifelessly at the poor attempt at consolation. This was certainly not going to be the last one. He felt nothing about it, and nothing about the god who adds and subtracts years to a person's life on whim.

When the rooms started to wear a familiar look of vacancy, he let his mind give in to more blasphemous tirade. To someone who had just lost a dear one, every cloud—even with a silver lining—is nothing but another obstruction to the life-giving sunlight.

The next day, after what seemed like the longest funeral—encased in a plain coffin, his father was lowered down into the grave in a silent farewell punctuated by loud outbursts of grief—Nzan found himself alone in the living room, staring blankly at his palms. They held nothing but the ghosts of many nameless handshakes from the day before. He moved his gaze up and looked around the room, and finally felt it settle upon a familiar object beside the TV. It was a board with rough, hand-drawn lines all over it—the scoreboard.

He picked it up and ran his fingers over the lines, stretching from one point to another, with a clear beginning

A Kite of Farewells

and end to their journey, intersecting and passing over other lines—so much like men's existence in this brief dance of entropy.

He noticed that his father had taken the liberty to fill up the scores right up to the final match. It read:

Uruguay (2) : Croatia (1)

Uruguay had lost to France by two goals the day before, and Croatia was yet to face Russia. The final was in a week and still courted many speculations. He wondered if he should strike off the earlier prediction and rewrite it with the corrected score, but decided against it after giving it some thought.

The scoreboard was more than itself—it embodied the stubborn hope of a dying man. His father had reached out into the future and played his last card at the table with fate.

Nzan got up and hung the scoreboard on the wall beside the only photo of his father in the room.

Eyes of the Tiger

*H*AVE YOU EVER STARED DEAD into the eyes of a tiger in the wilderness and let its piercing gaze—a blinding beam from an approaching car—consume you with the most absolute form of primal fear, defiling your soul and freezing your body on the very ground you stand on? I have had the fortune, or misfortune, in a not-so-distant past, of one such chance encounter, up in the hills of Jotsoma on a slumbering July night. It all started with a camping trip planned on a whim… but before that there was her.

She was no one to me then—and even now—in particular. She was a stranger, a pretty stranger, I took to fancying. Every morning, with the early sun peeking through the mist-topped hills surrounding Jotsoma, as I made my way up to Sir Choudhary's house for tuition, I saw her, with a book in her embrace, nonchalantly climbing up the flight of steps from her hostel, her nimble frame moving with grace. At times, we exchanged an awkward gaze that was at the cusp of a meek smile, but it went nowhere beyond that.

A Kite of Farewells

There was an unnerving yet alluring calmness in the way she carried herself, and although the notion of beauty is a subjective one best left to the judgement of the beholder, I can say that all my friends were unanimous in their verdict—she was 'different'.

'Selena from Section B'—that was what my friends called her, and still do to this day when she pops up occasionally in our evening beer-fuelled conversations.

In college, I would see her around the canteen during lunch with her clique, engrossed in a conversation that seemed dull from a distance. Days and months went by, and we both took to deriving comfort in each other's silent company as we ascended the same old, beaten road through gated hostels, half-timbered staff quarters, and rows of towering pine trees, towards our respective tuition teachers' residences. From the way she disappeared around the bend a little further down the crossroad, I supposed she was one of Sir Jha's physics tuition students. I never got around to knowing that either, but it is of little importance to the story.

I remember one incident during the annual Winter Fest where I struck up an 'almost conversation' with her. I was watching my friends sweat it out on the basketball court in a heated, deciding match between the two finalists, with her sitting across the court, arms crossed and eyes glued on the action. Whenever the court erupted with wild applause, I caught her stealing quick, sidelong glances at me every now and then, which made her pale face turn a flowery red and her fidgety hands fashion strands of her jet black hair into playful twirls. After the match came to an end, with both teams having had fought tooth and nail right up to the last round, I mustered all the courage in my reserve and made my way towards her, with a creepy smile on my face telling of my rather ambiguous intention. As I lifted my hand in a gesture of salutation, she suddenly turned her back to me and faced her friends in a conspicuous imitation of a busy conversation in progress. Taken aback, I put up a poor pretence of calling out, very publicly, to some Jimmy behind her, and disappeared into the short-lived anonymity of the crowd. My friends, to this day, make it a point to tease me with this incident whenever our conversations drift to the ever-blooming field of college nostalgia.

The last month of the academic year—and the last one before graduation—was drawing closer, and it was only a matter of time before we would be swamped with lab exams and assignment submissions. There were talks among the final-year students of going on a camping trip up the hills as a final act of camaraderie and also as 'something to look back on when we're old', as one of my usually reserved friends put it, inviting much appreciation. Every day in the class, talks of sublime nights under the stars increased in fervour, along with the number of claimants of such enviable adventure. 'I saw a tiger, crouched in the bushes and ready to pounce,' proclaimed one of the classmates who allegedly had a near-death encounter during his day out the previous week. It was an entertaining story but did little to dampen the general mood of the class, which was still making plans

A Kite of Farewells

and deciding a good day to bunk a day's worth of classes.

'Okay, everyone—next week!'

But which day of the week it was to be was left undecided and up for discussion when we met up after class at the bakery. There was something about the bakery—its state of general shabbiness, the overpowering smell of everything but baked goods, and the watery tea offered complimentary to us—that brought out long-winded debates, especially in the late evenings, about literally everything under the heavens, from outright nonsense to philosophical piffle. That evening, the conversation took a path somewhere in the comfortable middle between the two and finally came upon the camping plan. 'Some guys from Section B—my hostel mates—are leaving the day after tomorrow. What say we join them?' proposed one of my friends, and after a noisy round of back and forth, we decided that we would indeed be joining them on that day, the coming Friday.

On the said Friday, when the sun was inching up the sleepy hills, my friends and the guys from Section B met up at the junction that had surrendered itself to the eerie company of the humming wind, the shadowy spaces between the soulless buildings, and the idle yellow taxis parked haphazardly.

'Some girls from Leone hostel will be joining us,' said a short, unkempt guy from Section B hoarsely. After about fifteen minutes of waiting and making laughable efforts at small talks, I narrowed my eyes at the sight of four girls, their backpacks stuffed to full capacity, waving at us from a distance. There she was, struggling to keep a steady eye contact with us bunch of delighted guys grinning foolishly at each other.

The walk up to the mountains—through leech-riddled, damp grounds with overgrown shrubs and silvery blades of dew-kissed grass reaching up to the knee—was more exhausting than I had anticipated, and I found myself taking a minute every once in a while to catch a breath, trying to keep pace with the group seemingly on a mission to test the limits of human endurance.

The sun now had its salubrious swell of warm orange film over the canopies and the sweat-drenched faces of the hikers, and by the time we made our way to the top—an open ground with a commanding view—with me being the last, as expected, the day was making clear its intention of being a dry and sunny one. On the assurance that the water in the snaking creek below was 'clear as crystal', I took the liberty of draining the water bottle the moment my backpack hit the ground.

The aforementioned creek was a stone's throw away—I did remember throwing a pebble and hitting the water with a shy plop—and surrounded by arching tree branches dipping low into the lulling waters that flowed over moss-coated rocks. There was a waterfall ahead, an hour-and-a half walk away—or that's what I was told.

After a satisfying breakfast of lukewarm tea in plastic cups and sloppily buttered bread with a plateful of Popular Bakery's banana chips, we all sat in a circle and got to

A Kite of Farewells

making efforts at small talk with promising results: the four girls were reserved at first, limiting their participation to faint, self-conscious giggles and passing remarks here and there, but by the time we moved on to group games, they were taking solid initiatives on their own, manoeuvring the conversation from the all-enjoyable topic of 'who has a crush on whom' to more raucous ones best left undiscussed. Things soon took a noisier turn when bottles of whisky popped out of one guy's bag, and with the smoothness of a jazz band in the sombre moonlit hours, the wall of inhibitions came down brick by brick. The ease with which the girls swigged their shares made it evident that it was definitely not their first time.

She was away from the fun, under the rest house, performing inconspicuous poses for the waving Nokia 5800 pressed into the confident hand of one of the guys from Section B, some Kevi. Although she was posing with an apparent air of reluctance, something in her coquettish giggles gave an impression of things being otherwise. 'They are going out together,' remarked a friend when I nudged his attention towards the duo. Something inside me resisted that idea and my displeasure manifested as a low growl in my stomach, bordering on juvenile malice.

The hours leading up to the evening went by fast, unaccounted for but squeezed down to their last minute, and as the night fell slowly and majestically upon our tired eyes, we lit a roaring bonfire to welcome the last bit of the day's quota of entertainment. With steaming cups of tea in our cold hands, we sat shoulder to shoulder around the fire bartering stories of an extravagantly comical variety, occasionally interrupted with banter and always met with peals of laughter, irrespective of the content of the narration. I suspect the booze—the last bottle, as declared—had something to do with the majority's blurry sense of humour, but who am I to judge? I myself gave in, in the heat of the moment, to a generous sip of the dark brown liquid; not my first, but it was more than enough to get me tipsy.

'You know, they saw a tiger lurking not far from here last week,' said a guy from Section B when the conversation was running dry from a dire exhaustion of topics. It was met with cold shrugs and half-assed nods. Eventually we found ourselves crawling back to our tents, mighty exhausted and inebriated, clutching at the evaporating warmness in our jackets as soon as the last drop of kerosene ran out in the waning, stubs-strewn bonfire. And right before I was to retire for the night into my tent along with three of my friends, for a long, hard sleep, I looked around to take in the sight of the night and all of its offerings for the last time. A thing about being in the mountains—among the wilderness and surrendered to nature—is that no matter the season, be it the harshest of the summer or the cruellest of the winter, the nights bring out a certain resilience in its dwellers—a primal instinct to put one's survival above everything else. But that night, except for the ringing chorus of crickets, the forest seemed bare and lonely, until his eyes fixed on something familiar.

A Kite of Farewells

In the distance, their faces cloaked by the night, Selena and the guy with the Nokia phone sat in the resting shed, their arms like tentacles around each other, looking at the shimmering lights of the town below. It was pretty evident at that point that they were very much dating and more. A strange, stomach-turning feeling seared through my insides, presenting itself this time as a mild arrhythmia of the senses arrested in an irresolvable suspense—making a mockery of one's affection. It was envy making itself known. A part of me wanted to strangle the guy into submission. But I restrained myself, swallowed a sentence of the vilest combination of words, and promptly disappeared into the tent for the loneliest sleep of my life.

After what I suppose were two hours, I woke up drenched in sweat and needing urgent bladder relief. The night then was no different than the night I had abandoned two hours ago; only this time it was less inviting of a stroll in the bushes regardless of one's business. I sheepishly tip-toed my way down, lighted by the screen of my tiny Samsung phone, towards an arching bush waving in the wind. Without hesitation, I emptied the liquid wobbling inside my bladder onto the dry roots of the bush. But before I was fully relieved, I was interrupted by the rustling of dry leaves, telling of a certain wild prowler from the stories. *Oh please let it not be a tiger*, I prayed. The hair on my arms, feet and everything in between stood up in electric attention, and with my zipper still open in all its glory, my foot was ready for flight for survival. But for some inexplicable reason, rivalling the kind of curiosity that killed the cat, I decided to probe the origin of the sound, notwithstanding my fear-soaked self. I deftly pushed the leaves of the bush away, just enough to qualify for a peek, and threw the light of my phone's screen on—fortunately not a tiger—a couple in an act of lovemaking. The weak light from the phone's screen fell on the bare buttocks of a guy arrested in motion, about to thrust at the lady whose legs were wrapped around his—there she was, Selena from Section B, caught in that feeble light, to my utmost horror.

Upon sensing my obvious intrusion, her gaze locked on the pale light emanating from the other side of the bush; her eyes were fiery, almost tiger-like. For some time I stood still like I had finally met the fabled tiger from the stories, building momentum to get myself out of the scene. When the senses finally roared back to life, I fled like a madman, but not before I blurted a quick, 'I am so sorry.' It was pretty obvious that the lady with the tiger eyes, Selena, figured out at that very instant from my voice that it was me who had caught them in the middle of the deed.

Later in the tent, as I tossed violently from side to side, I swear that I heard faint moaning floating into the tent, but my imagination was haywire.

The next morning's walk down—after the usual hassle of scampering around for the near-perfect group picture—was quicker than I anticipated, with me following last, this time intentionally, to steer clear of the risk of locking eyes with the lady with tiger eyes and her accomplice from last

A Kite of Farewells

night. No sooner had I made my way down and sighted the junction ahead, still wearing a deserted look, I took leave from the group and stole away to my hostel, taking extra precautions not to let my eyes stray too far ahead.

The next week, as I made my way up the road to my tuition teacher's residence, I sensed something amiss—the sight of Selena climbing the steps from her hostel with a notebook in her embrace. The days following that were no good either, and by the month's end, it was clear that she had switched to a different batch, probably the evening one, or had abandoned the tuition altogether. With no other choice, I got comfortable with the fact that from then on, it would be just me and my playlist of British pop bangers on the long, empty morning walks, which admittedly turned out to be not so bad, as my taste in music grew by leaps and bounds.

◆

College farewells, they say, should not be taken for granted, for they may very well be your last shared moment before your friends disappear into the rat race, to emerge worn out and sucked out of all joy, only to meet again in the helpless despair of hospital rooms or at short-notice funerals, with a wealth of words to share but, alas, late by just a mere moment.

I was gripped by a similar sentiment when I saw her standing with a bouquet of red roses, looking at the passing crowd. But giving in to better judgement, I hesitated approaching her. I stood there for the longest moment, and

Eyes of the Tiger

imprinted the lonely, lovely sight of her in the pixels of my memory, letting it slip silently under the shifting currents of my subconscious, with those tiger eyes stirring my senses like they did the night I chanced upon her, young and reckless, prowling the haunting landscapes of primal passion.

That was the last time I saw Selena from Section B, and the eyes of the tiger.

The Encyclopaedia Salesman

I HAVE ALWAYS BEEN FASCINATED WITH encyclopaedias—with the captivating illustrations and the plethora of information inside their pages, so much so that I ended up selling stocks of them for a living, but I swear that the decision was mostly an economical one and not so much an act of unbridled passion.

I'd be lying if I claimed to have seen anyone who'd say that they enjoyed the act, or the art if I may, of going around the neighbourhood, darkening many a door in the prospect of making a quick sale. A sale or two a day buys the next day's dinner (to be frank, calling it a dinner would be overstretching the definition a tad bit). The things a man must do to get by, a single day at a time, squaring his existence into a convenient intersection of budget and pride, or whatever little is left of it...

This unholy pursuit of selling encyclopaedias has taken

The Encyclopaedia Salesman

me into the intimate spaces of many houses, and in between the pauses of my rehearsed pitch I would take pleasure in scrutinizing the lives of the many people inhibiting those beaten spaces.

I have seen the rich and their antique faux-Victorian furniture with cabriole legs; cabinets housing memorabilia and souvenirs of ivory, cabochon stones and pristine porcelain; ever-ubiquitous tufted sofa sets of lush velvet; Persian rugs sprawled in invitation of noble reveries; walls with framed accomplishments humbling and mocking their observers at the same time. The poor, contrary to expectation, showed some variety in their restrained offerings: there were new TV sets with stickers still on, perhaps to convey a sense of sustained newness; dual-toned, government-issued calendars alongside other calendars emblazoned with names of unions and organizations; and occasionally a mirage of opulence in the form of second-hand curtains with garish embroideries and crockery sets telling of diligent hands polishing it after the guests make their farewell.

But some sad sights plagued the poor and the rich alike, like absent fathers and distant mothers, with an insatiable hunger for accumulation of stuff to compensate for the much-needed attention demanded of them by their children when they were growing up.

By the time I walked out the door, I would have a colourful page or two in my intangible encyclopaedia of people. And when there was nothing to do in my one-room rented house, I would concoct an absurd story from the

A Kite of Farewells

many characters populating this imaginary encyclopaedia.

This particular house stood out from a distance, flanked by a thatched house and a half-wall brick house. Its high walls around the perimeter told of a man who wanted little or nothing to do with the usual business of the colony. This was the last house before the conclusion of the day's business, and I frankly didn't expect much more than a stern 'no' from the owner at the very outset.

I made my way inside through the gate, which screeched and wailed on movement, and through the rows of immaculate calla lilies and peeping bougainvillea. The walk through the flowery display induced a calming effect.

I found myself seated in the common room conversing with the owner: a soft-spoken retired government officer in his late sixties who instantaneously took a liking to my encyclopaedias, which was unusual because men of his status, with a career of bossing around subordinates, were more inclined to be loud in their admission of suspicion and disinterest in things that challenged and subverted their sphere of command. What annoyed such men more was the vague possibility that for once in their life they would be hoodwinked by a lesser man like me. It would amount to an abominable upset of social order.

'Show me the one about medieval history,' instructed the host.

'Sure, Amo. Give me a moment to get them out of my bag.'

'Okay, while you are at it, I shall run to the kitchen and get us some grape juice. Do you mind?' he offered.

The Encyclopaedia Salesman

'That would be great, especially in this heat,' I obliged.

I got out the encyclopaedia of medieval history and placed it on the table. In the course of waiting for my host to return, I let my eyes wander around the sitting room to pass the time. It showed all the usual trappings of a well-lived life—an exotic porcelain vase inside the wall cabinet alongside volumes of lofty literature, exquisite bottles of French-sounding wine emptied over many late-night talks among learned company. I say, here was a man who had lived a great life.

My eyes, awed and intrigued, settled on the wall of framed photos arranged in the form of a tree in full bloom—on a particular photo of a beaming woman in her graduation garb. A sense of ancient familiarity came over me. I got up from the sofa and walked towards it to soak in the details of the photo.

'This can't be true…'

A faint yelp of excitement escaped my mouth as the slow rush of an old memory flooded my mind.

'Oh, that's my daughter.' The host walked into the room holding a tray with two glass cups filled with grape juice to the brim. 'Mimi.'

'She is a dentist now, running her own clinic in Kohima,' he continued.

All my silent questions stood answered.

'That's great,' I remarked.

'Don't tell me you sold her an encyclopaedia too?' he asked jokingly.

A Kite of Farewells

'I might have, Amo. It's a small world.' Little did he know I gave her something much more than that.

There was a time in my life when I knew her—we dated for half a year when I was in Delhi for my studies.

'Things do come around in this small, no-name town,' I thought aloud.

I still remember her eyes: they were exquisite and intense. Under their gaze you felt lavished with a kind of attention that trickled down to the bones. However, when you crossed her, those eyes were most unforgiving. Besides the eyes, I don't recall much of her face, maybe except her nose, and how it crinkled when she smiled.

'And what about a discount?' the host asked.

With my eyes flirting between the photo and the host, I tried to make a just division of my attention. So as not to arouse any suspicion, I squeezed in a passing remark about the items in the room to present myself as one who is a curious observer of his environment, which the host greatly appreciated and entertained.

Below her graduation picture was another picture of her beaming at the beach, wearing a straw hat and a polka sundress. It must have been exactly what she dreamt of—the beach.

She always talked about wanting to go to the beach, and in our many hours of conversations, she would joyously lay out the nitty-gritty of her possible beach escapade in the future.

So what went wrong?

Time.

The Encyclopaedia Salesman

'We don't always want the same thing over time.' A precocious presage of her invention, which has come to sit comfortably with me as time passed. I don't even recall the circumstance that elicited those words, and the mind is a dark alley to walk down in search of a faint memory after the storm of consequences had blown over. Some stories just are to be remembered in their conclusion, for there is an arcane wisdom in ignorance sometimes.

I came back to have a crack at exams, and with each successive failure and closed doors, I lost sight of the horizon where she beckoned in that faraway land. Eventually, one day everything just stopped—just like that.

And the strange thing was that I felt nothing when it all ended. It was as if the writing had been on the wall all along.

My last memory of her was at the airport. Before I boarded my flight, I had pushed into her hand a framed picture of a shoddy illustration I had made of her the week before—my farewell gift. I was not one to give in to grand gestures, but I felt that was the least I could do to show my appreciation for the love she had lavished on my poor soul. She politely accepted—she generally disliked gifts—and hugged me, sharing our last moment of togetherness in comfortable silence.

'I will buy the medieval and the geography ones,' said the host.

I quickly wrote him the cash memo and signed over the books to him.

A Kite of Farewells

After the transaction, I hurriedly stuffed the other books inside my bag and proceeded to make my way out. There was something outside I was impatient to see, so my act of pacing turned into prancing.

Just as I was nearing the end of the corridor that seemed to stretch for an eternity, I caught a glimpse of something that stopped me dead in my tracks. From the door that was ajar, leading inside to a room of possibly feminine occupancy, I could see this vaguely discernible framed photo of a familiar illustration—the shoddy sketch that I had gifted to her at the airport. I walked two steps forward to luxuriate in the privilege of that sight. After all these years, she had kept it.

It had been so long since I felt that warm, fuzzy feeling coursing through my being.

◆

At the gate, on the verge of walking out, I turned back to the house—to the roof—scanning its vicinity for a wooden or a steel ladder; an old, musty thing pressed against one of the walls found my eyes. In our many conversations, she would talk about struggling to get to the roof—it offered better network coverage—on a shaky ladder, and how getting down from the roof was trickier.

A few minutes away from the gate, and the surprising turn of events that had transpired started to weigh less heavily on me as the gnawing teeth of reality sunk in. The house from the distance also assumed a look of sameness

The Encyclopaedia Salesman

like the others dotting the expanse. Yet another moated castle of comfort.

For a lesser man like me, love is a luxury I can't afford. Matters of the heart play second fiddle to the shrieking struggle for mere survival, and with the profit from the two encyclopaedias that I just sold, I had enough to face tomorrow with renewed hope. And hope is more valuable than gold and silver for people like me.

Showroom

I AM NOT SOMEONE WHO FREQUENTS showrooms, and it is for a rather simple but unusual reason: something about them makes me feel inadequate.

The proportion-perfect mannequins staring out from the storefronts clad in immaculate fashion; the room-sized posters of spectacularly sculpted models flashing their pearly teeth; the squeaky clean, tiled floor polished to a slippery shine; the mechanical attendants tailing you around the aisles armed with the most refined brand of courteousness; the soul-stripping dressing rooms reflecting every flaw back at you; the sophisticated shoppers who go about with an air of elegance, sifting through the displays and making witty remarks about the materials; the invasive smile on the face of the cashier judging your every purchase.

I shop cheap and had been doing so unapologetically for as long as I could remember.

There was this new showroom in PR Hill, which opened a month ago to much fanfare—the proprietor had bought a full-page spread in all the local dailies for a full week prior to the opening day. The showroom—one giant building with four floors—sold high-end, branded apparel and footwear with hefty price tags.

In the evenings when I go out to buy groceries from the merry Lotha women seated in rows under one of the overbridges, I would pass by the showroom, the evening sun reflecting off the storefront, always swarming with shoppers. During one such evening, I saw a queue starting from its wide entrance and spilling out onto the sidewalk. Plastered over the storefront were posters in bright red—SALE: 50% OFF.

The queue moved in lurches, and with the entry of each person, the metal detector positioned in front of the glass swing-door emitted a loud beep. The frequency of the beeps and the subsequent shuffling of feet lent a strange rhythm to the whole thing.

I remember having this weird dream about walking into the showroom with all my uncivilized manners and being the lone soul inside, running from one long aisle to another like a rat caught in a maze, desperate to get out. I woke up screaming, and after it dawned on me that it was just a nightmare, I laid on my bed and laughed like a madman till my mouth started to hurt. The next day as I passed by the showroom, a cold, stabbing fear took hold of me and I felt an inexplicable urge to run away from it.

In the office during lunch, as I was unpacking my tiffin—inside it the usual rice, dal and alu fry—I saw a paper carry bag with the logo of the showroom laid on the table of my

A Kite of Farewells

office-cubicle mate. Based on the limited interactions I have had with him over the span of a year working together, he seemed like a nice chap: the kind this workplace chews up and spits out in a nauseous cycle by the dozens. It's a surprise that he still somehow managed to bring in every morning an outlook of optimism, with no visible signs of fatigue, even though he was drawing a pittance of a salary. I suppose some people are either just too easy to please or good at pretending to be content. Either way, that is an issue of no immediate bearing on me. I pointed at the paper bag and said in a flat tone:

'That paper bag...'

Well, it doesn't take a genius to figure that one out.

'Yes, paper bag?' he asked in a sarcastic tone.

'Bought something at the new showroom?' I asked.

'Nothing special. Just a pullover. It was on sale.' He reached for the bag. 'You wanna see?'

'Well, if you insist.'

I could hear a chuckle running down my throat.

I ran my fingers across the fine details of the bag: the extra-large, eye-catching logo in the brightest red known to science; the noisy texture of its print; the crispy thickness of the paper material; the sharp creases formed under pressure that gave it some semblance of a character. I had little to no interest in the contents of the bag: one grey sweatshirt with the repulsive aesthetics of an old coal miner's sweat after a long day of work. In that moment, I pictured myself walking out of the showroom—without a hint of apprehension—with a similar bag, waving it gleefully in a tribal celebration of pure triumph. I was so intrigued that I decided to make my showroom shopping debut in a week.

'It's the best-looking sweatshirt I have seen in my life.' A bold lie of course.

I handed back the paper bag without looking at him.

'But you barely even opened it,' he said.

'I know quality when I see it.' Another shameless lie.

I was, without any doubt, the best liar in the whole damn office.

The following days, I ran probable scenarios—mostly favourable—inside my head about the big debut. I rehearsed them diligently before sleep and in the early morning; every line I could say to the attendants on that fateful day was put under scrutiny like lines from an esoteric play. I also made contingency plans in case a moment slipped past me unaware and jeopardized my laboured sense of routine. I made a mental map from images collected online of the showroom, of its many aisles and counters. I was prepped like a soldier embarking on a secret world-saving mission. Now the only thing needed to push me into action was a dab of courage, and perhaps a shot of vodka.

My sentences start to drag out into a comical stutter when I am nervous, and alcohol, on many occasions, seems to help the case by keeping my conversation lean. The only shortcoming is that I tend to lose grip on reality, and civilized predisposition, when under the influence of alcohol. The thought of having my uncouth aggression captured on one

A Kite of Farewells

of those tiny CCTVs inside made alcohol strongly a non-option—also my monthly budget was in shambles and made a decent drink unaffordable.

One evening while I was returning with a bag of edible silkworms—a pay-day extravaganza—I happened to pass by the showroom and was gripped by this sudden urge to walk in. I stood still for a moment to assess the place. The usual traffic swarming the place was amiss, which further intensified my desire. I walked up the flight of stairs leading to the entrance and stood two steps away from the metal detector. The watch-woman, upon seeing me, motioned at me from behind the glass door to step through the metal detector. A loud beep, a swing of the door, a delightful smile from the watch-woman, and I was inside, facing a labyrinth of aisles, carrying a blue polythene bag with shifting, live silkworms inside. A cold shiver of panic crawled down my spine. I tartly turned back towards the entrance in a flight reflex. Another assistant, a baby-faced, twenty-something guy, approached me and said: 'Sir, you need to deposit your bag at that counter.' He then pointed his pudgy finger to a counter manned by two neatly dressed ladies with a smile that looked uncanny.

After handing over the bag and getting a token in return, I hesitantly disappeared into the aisles. I was in awe of the assortment of choices: rows and rows of tagged branded products in varied forms and hues pristinely hanging from metallic hangers. As I stood transfixed, I felt a light tap on my shoulder from behind. I turned around to the beaming

Showroom

face of another attendant, who promptly asked me: 'Sir, can I help you in finding what you are looking for?'

I took a moment to collect my thoughts but found none too convincing, so I simply pointed at the mannequin in front of me and said: 'That.'

The attendant scratched his neatly combed head and replied, 'Sir, you can find T-shirts like that to the right.'

'Yes, T-shirts, like that, umm... Thank you.'

I brushed my hand through the long racks packed with T-shirts, each more desirable than the last one, turning over the labels at a suspicious frequency to check the price—it was apparent that I was walking out empty-handed if I didn't find something with a price tag well within my budget soon.

On seeing another attendant walking by, I asked him:

'Where are the things on sale?'

'It's over there.' I swear I noticed some disdain when he spoke those words.

My eyes followed his finger to an almost bare rack with a bright red sign declaring: SALE: BUY 1 GET 2 FREE. Aha! I might be buying something after all.

Satisfied with the price tag and the offer that presumably came along with it, I handed over a white tote bag with the logo of the showroom printed on it to the attendant.

'I will take four of these please,' I declared.

The attendant quickly looked at me with an animated look of confusion.

'But sir, these,' he lowered her voice, 'are carry bags we give for free to every shopper. We hang these here along with the price tags misplaced from the innerwear section.'

My face turned red with hot, fuming panic.

Without losing a beat, to the mounting astonishment of the attendants, and without giving much thought to the words shaping in my mouth, I blurted, 'Where is the trial room?'

She took a moment to compose herself. Her eyes were screaming with laughter, and she was making pronounced effort to subdue it.

Inside the trial room, with the silly white tote bag slung over my shoulder, I stared at the buffoon cluelessly looking back at me in the mirror.

'I should get out ASAP,' I concluded.

'Sir, would you like a bag for your—bags?' asked the cashier.

'Umm...yes?' Coherent sentences were escaping me by then.

She gave a sidelong glance to the other girl and raised her eyebrows. After a quick minute of typing the cash memo out, she handed me my bags—inside a slightly bigger bag. It was paid all in cash: four hundred rupees. The cheapest transaction since its opening. I thanked the cashier, and the other cashier, and the attendant, and then hurriedly proceeded towards the exit. But then I remembered something—

'What in god's name?!' shouted a lady customer with a blue polythene bag in her hands—my blue polythene bag, with silkworms inside.

Showroom

'That's mine, Miss.' I yanked it away from her grip. She looked at me with the most disgusting feature conceivable on a human face.

Without offering any explanation, I ran towards the exit, the sound of my nervous footsteps upon the squeaky-clean floor inviting more unsolicited attention from the amused staff and the shoppers.

As I descended the flight of stairs outside, I heard roars of wild laughter echo through the showroom's aisles, lift towards the glass-panelled ceiling, and spill out onto the busy street from the ventilators. I ran with my back against it till the air inside my lungs started to thicken.

Ever since that day, I buy my groceries from a place that is a twenty-minute taxi ride away from the showroom, and frequent second-hand clothing stores with a particular white tote bag slung over my shoulder.

Page 59

As far as I could see, even with my eyes squinted, nothing but untainted whiteness stretched into the furthest distance. The sky was crystal clear, without the sun or an avian intruder in sight. It seemed perfect, too perfect.

After walking for about an hour, my confusion compounding with every counting step, something beckoned in the horizon: a shimmering dot in an ocean of maddening whiteness. As I covered the distance with the enthusiasm of a child running towards an ice cream van, that dot started to assume form: a jaggy dash, a rigid box, and eventually a nauseous brutalist monolith of a building with a single monstrous entrance and without a single window. Its grey facade imposing over me made me question the sigh of relief I felt a while ago when its silhouette bent to the contours of my hopeful despair. I stood still for a moment and took in the scale and skewness of its form. Its sheer enormity and tepidity assaulted my senses.

Two steps inside the building, through the hitherto motionless revolving glass door, I was overwhelmed by the deluge of business happening inside its four walls—or six; it was hard to tell. Clad in sombre grey suits with emaciated faces sticking out of immaculately ironed collars and wearing the bluest of blue neckties, everyone carried themselves with a sense of otherworldly hurriedness. The people in grey suits were racing from one end to another, appearing from and disappearing into one of the many doors opening into the grand lobby.

I walked up to one of them and tapped him on the shoulder. He turned towards me, scanned me from top to bottom, and succinctly announced:

'Top of the stairs. Room number one. Knock before entering.'

'Excuse me?' I asked, hoping to get a better explanation.

'There—' He pointed curtly at the stairs leading from the reception.

On my ascent, I caught a glimpse of the said door. It was much bigger than the other doors and had a distinctive golden doorknob. All the others had the same white knob.

I knocked on the door and waited for a voice from inside. But upon hearing nothing for the next five minutes, I let myself in and found myself staring at the ceiling— or lack thereof—and the sheer magnificence of the rapid psychedelic swirls of shifting colours unknown to my earthly eyes. Underneath the glory of it all sat a tiny man in the same grey suit and blue tie, hunched over his tidy desk, furiously writing something on his notepad. On the edge of the table was a golden nameplate. It read: *The Almighty God*.

A Kite of Farewells

Before I could fully register the shock of this strange presentation, I found myself sitting down on a leather chair that had materialized out of thin air, facing the tiny man who was now earnestly looking at me, as if in anticipation of the words to come out of my mouth.

'Are y-you—?' I stuttered.

'Absolutely not. Nobody is almighty or the Almighty,' he replied.

'But the ceiling, and the nameplate?'

'It is what it is. And no, I am not God,' he assured me.

I took a moment to look around again. The room had grown in proportion with stacks of files strewn all over the place now. Some of the stacks were so enormous that they reached up to the ceiling and beyond it, punching through the swirling mass of colours, moving now with increased agitation.

'Does this mean that I am dead or something?'

'Most certainly. Oh, where are my manners? I am Barry.' He took my hand and shook it.

'This is ridiculous. I am dead and talking to God, umm, Barry.'

He nodded at me.

'I just keep the nameplate for giggles. The one before you broke out into hymns and started bawling.'

'Tell you what—' He leaned forward.

'Since you will be here for the next—' He checked his watch, '—fifteen minutes, why don't I entertain all the questions inside that head of yours, Noel? It's Noel, right?'

Page 59

I nodded in affirmation.

'What happens after fifteen minutes?' I asked.

'That you will know when you know. Besides, going by the manual, I am not supposed to tell you even if I knew.'

'Manual?' I asked.

'About that, later. Do you want to ask about something more substantial? Like, how I got the name Barry?'

'Alright, please tell.'

'I gave it to myself.' He seemed unimpressed with his own words.

'You gave it yourself?' I asked out of politeness.

'I don't remember being given a name, or even being born for that matter. One fine day I was blinked into existence here. Adult, fully formed, and among this mountain of files. I fancied myself a name after seeing you folks walking in with names, each more unique and endearing than the other. Barry sounded right in the moment, so I stuck with it.'

'What about those men outside in grey suits and blue ties?' I asked.

'They are my agents, but I think you earthlings call them angels, or something like that. Here, inside our establishment, they are the clerks, the indispensable cogs in the great unending cosmic machinery of obscure function some call heaven, or purgatory, or even hell.'

'They certainly look more elegant and daintier in old paintings and movies,' I remarked to his amusement.

'The laudable ingenuity of humans: ascribing noble values and aspirations to things beyond their comprehension.

A Kite of Farewells

I guess there is some comfort in assuring oneself that one could grasp the unknowable.'

He roared with laughter that echoed through the entire building. It was an unnerving experience.

'So, Barry, what exactly is your role in this establishment?' I persisted with the questions.

'I am more of what you normally call a manager. You see this book?' He pointed at a thick book with suede leather cover; it had the word 'Manual' written on it.

'I simply follow the instructions written on it. They magically appear and disappear by the hour.'

'Appear and disappear?' I asked.

'Yeah, it's a different instruction every time.'

'What if you don't follow it?'

'Now that is a luxury I can't afford. You see the stacks of files over there?' He pointed toward the far end of the room. In the few minutes I was in the room, the stacks had grown in scale like they could topple any moment.

'We are extremely understaffed, and at the rate at which we are getting footfall these days, I wouldn't be surprised to have these stacks of files for a table and a chair any day soon.'

He let out a faint laughter, which was anything but amusing this time; it carried a tone of misery, the likes of which I had heard often from overworked, blue-collared folks.

'Did you try to do something about it?' I asked.

'Well, some aeons ago, me and the managers from the other establishments got together to form a mega union to demand better hours and working conditions.'

'Other establishments?' I asked.

'Oh I'm sorry, you don't know that yet. Yes, there are other buildings like this one. Us managers get together occasionally to barter stories.'

'So did the mega union thing work out?'

'Unfortunately no. We had our demands straight but were not sure about whom to direct these to. We were like bushmen dancing around a fire for rain; something is definitely out there dictating it all, but anything beyond that information is unsure. There was no booming heavenly voice or manifestation of a mighty power. Silence—nothing but deafening silence. It was humiliating to say the least. We called it off shortly and never spoke of it again.'

'What about the staff? Do they know about this?'

'Yes. They are under as much stress as I am. And as much as I would like to demand more from their schedule, I have to tread carefully by their union's guidelines.'

'Wait, they have a union too?'

'Well, it seems the most logical way to safeguard one's interests, so why not? It's ironic that an institution like ours is no different from an earthly one—crippled by the banality of bureaucracy.'

He paused.

'But, you know, at the end of the day, we've got to get things done amidst all the disgruntlement and frustration.'

A hurried knocking was heard, followed by a taut voice.

'Sir, Gilbert here. It's the report.'

'Come in, Gilbert. I was expecting you,' Barry called out

A Kite of Farewells

to the person behind the door.

A man in the same sullen garb walked in. He had a mild smile on his face. It looked rehearsed. He proceeded to place the report on the table and stood in attention awaiting the next word from Barry.

Barry, after pouring over the report, looked up and pointed at the stack of files.

'Gilbert, file no. BV69182.'

Without missing a beat, Gilbert paced over to one of the stacks of files and began rummaging through it.

'Sir,' he called out after some time, 'there seems to be some ambiguity.'

I could hear a strain of despair in his voice.

'I will check on it in a moment,' said Barry and turned his attention to me again.

'Hey, you obviously must have noticed the swirling ceiling by now. I was inspired by how humans would decorate their boring cubicles with photographs and trinkets to make the space a little more tolerable. I like to think it worked.'

Barry got up from his chair to disappear into the stack of files, and I looked up at the ceiling again. He was right: in the ocean of drab monotony, it lent a sense of chaotic excitement.

After a noisy shuffling of feet and flutter of pages, Barry emerged out of the stacks with a grey file in hand.

'Got it!' he exclaimed. 'Gilbert, you may leave now.'

As the door closed behind Gilbert, Barry laid the file on the table and proceeded to carefully study its content.

Page 59

'Alright, it's good to go then. In about a minute, a door will open to your left. Your destination awaits you there,' he proclaimed.

'What will I find there?' I asked.

'Frankly, I am as curious as you are, but I am afraid I don't really know.'

He reached for the manual on the table, flipped through it, and stopped on a page.

'Here, Page 59 of the manual says, "The door reveals what it hides."'

'That doesn't help me much.' I shrugged at him.

Whoosh! A door materialized to my left.

Barry motioned me to walk through it.

I stood with my hand on the knob and looked around the room for the last time. The stacks of files seemed to have spawned more such, as these now occupied a good half of the room. Barry looked miserable in spite of the gaiety of the ceiling above his head.

'Barry,' I called out, 'you have a nice day.'

'I haven't heard that in a long time. You too, Noel.'

As I closed the door behind me in anticipation of the next thing to come, I heard someone knocking on Barry's door and the faint voice of Barry asking the person to come in.

The last light disappeared into the closing gap of the door, and I stood facing the mouth of darkness, the likes of which I had never known. It was endless; it seemed to be moving like it was alive.

A Kite of Farewells

I mustered all the courage in my reserve and walked towards it.

When I came face to face with it, it swept over me, fusing with the atoms of my being, after which I became one with it. Suddenly, I knew everything and saw everything, an entire lifetime in a blink of an eye, until my world was once again consumed by darkness.

Then I was sucked into a tunnel with light bursting through the other end.

When my eyes met the blinding lights at the other end, a voice like that of an angel whispered into my ears: 'My beloved.'

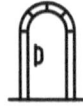

About a Chair

'HE HAD BEEN CRYING OUT *for help all along.*'

Vivi had just moved into one of the new housing colonies in the outskirts of Narengi, not far from her new college. Having cleared the state board exams two months ago, she had boarded a train to Guwahati and found herself lost in the insomniac blur of city life. It took her considerable time to warm up to its towering buildings, the busy, wide roads, and the pervasive loneliness that comes with such atomized existence. She grew numb to the city's vacuous glitz but didn't yearn for home. She knew that back at home, in Nagaland, she couldn't have something she had now in abundance—peace.

Three years ago, her father, a raging alcoholic, was caught in bed with a girl no older than Vivi, by one of her aunts. Ever since that day, a high-voltage drama had seized the household. To add fuel to fire, her aunt made sure that everyone in the colony knew of the scandal by bringing it up at whim. Vivi suspected it had more to do with her aunt's

A Kite of Farewells

not-so-secret spite for her. Her father, after a long spell of denial, got physically abusive whenever he felt cornered into admission.

Through all of it—nights of staring into the mouth of nothingness—a tiny voice in the back of her head grew and lifted to a crescendo.

It was reason, and it said only one thing:

'Get away.'

At the station, her brother, a clerk trainee at the PWD office, saw her off. It was a cold morning and the air inside the station smelt foul; it probably had something to do with all the refuse of civilization gratuitously littered around the tracks. As the train hissed and clanged onwards, she looked out at her brother feebly waving at her; his eyes said everything that could never be said in words.

This was not her first time in Guwahati: when she had been in class nine, her class won an excursion trip to Guwahati on account of their annual school performance. Much of the details about the trip remain hazy now, but she remembered being amazed at the scale of things when she got out of the station—everything, including the rats, looked bigger. The group photo in Pan Bazaar on the last day came out in one of the local newspapers, but since the school was hesitant about spending more on the coverage, it took a lot of deduction to figure out who was who in the black-and-white thumb-sized photo.

♦

About a Chair

'No loud music after nine,' declared the landlord when they signed the rent agreement. Vivi would be sharing the apartment with two other girls.

The landlord—Dada, as they would come to address him—was a mild-mannered corporate retiree who often disappeared for a month or two to attend to his business somewhere in Kerala. There were talks around the colony that he was running an alcohol syndicate involving big names, but it seemed incredulous for a man as docile as him to be at the helm of such an operation.

The 'no loud music after nine' rule did not hold out for too long after two guys from the same college moved into the opposite apartment. Dada also started to care less about it when the initial warning knocks on the door lost their persuasive authority. The guys paid their rent on time, and it did no one good to court unnecessary drama late in the night. On the weekends, when the peeved wife would nag him to knock some senses into the heads of the guys, Dada would make his way up the stairs, only to scurry back after some time with a pint tucked inside his shirt. Needless to say, he appeared to be a man who knew how much petty nuisances are worth in the market.

◆

Everything would fall into place and make sense for a while in the evenings when she sat out on the balcony with a book and waited for the night to try and lull the people winding down after a stressful day at work. She noticed

A Kite of Farewells

that some people, seduced by the prospect of bigger riches, never seemed to sleep.

One such evening, her listless pondering was interrupted by the dry creaking of a wooden chair emanating from the opposite apartment separated by a one-lane road. On a balcony quite like Vivi's, a guy sat rocking the wooden chair with a book held to his face. The smoke of the cigarette in his other hand snaked up to his head like the creepers on the pipe leading from the balcony to the gutter below. Even from that distance, the book jacket was unmistakable: *The Fountain of Eternal Discontent* by the controversial Ladong McBig. As he set the book down on the stool, she got a glimpse of his face—a good-looking one with a prominent chin and obviously from the Northeast as evidenced from his eyes—but she couldn't place her finger on which part of the Northeast he might be from.

Her coy scrutiny, however, was interrupted by the ungodly screeching of the rickety chair he sat on.

The chair, with its one leg bent like a bow, looked like it had not been put to much use by the owner. It used to sit out in the balcony collecting dust before this stranger decided to put his faith in the worn-out build of the chair by throwing his entire weight onto it. Surprisingly, it held its own under the weight, but something about the rusty nails sticking out of the joints said that it may give out anytime soon.

So for many evenings to follow, while she sat with a book on the balcony, she would keep an ear out for the dry

About a Chair

creaking of the chair. It started to grow on her so much so that she was more thrilled than annoyed by it, for it assured her of the silent company of the stranger, whom she would steal a quick look at every now and then from the corner of her eyes. He would reciprocate in the same way. But she also didn't expect the shy exchange to blossom into anything concrete.

When the night crept in, the stranger would flick away his cigarette with panache and drag the chair back into his room. He would then shut the door to the balcony with a thud.

◆

It was a sunny Sunday morning when one of her roommates, Toli, came back to the apartment with a guy she had met a week ago at a house-warming party. The guy was from the same apartment as the stranger on the balcony. Over a cup of tea hurriedly made by Toli, the guy told Vivi that the stranger on the balcony—one of his roommates—was called Clement.

He also added that this Clement guy was quite the character. He had a brooding predisposition and was awfully private about his life. The guy joked that they see him only twice a day: during lunch and dinner.

One evening, two chapters into a novel she had picked up out of boredom, Vivi sensed something amiss—the company of the stranger on the balcony, Clement. The familiar sound of the chair creaking was replaced by the

A Kite of Farewells

intermittent honking of scooters and hatchbacks zipping through the road below. She pressed the page into a crease and walked to the edge of the balcony. With her person leaning against the railing, she scanned the balcony opposite and its desolate offering.

For the first time, she felt her eyes rest on the mouldy walls, the paint peeling off in odd places giving it some semblance of deliberate design. As her eyes drifted over the walls to the finer details of the building, she also came to an uneasy realization: this stranger, by his conspicuous absence that evening, had made her aware of his essentiality to her routine. And with that revelation, she felt the world shrink into the liminal space between fact and fiction. Suddenly, she was seized with a feeling that she once felt when she was a teenager. Then the swift arrow of reality cut short the lofty ascent of her train of thoughts and jolted her back to her senses and to the tragic possibility that Clement was gone without a proper goodbye.

◆

'Do you know where Clement is?' Vivi asked.

Toli's guy friend from last month's Sunday, now promoted to a boyfriend, took a minute to remember the face of the stranger—Vivi's—cornering him, with bags full of groceries, in one of the aisles of the supermarket.

'Oh, you're Vivi.' He certainly took his time trying to recall her face. 'Clement left last week without notice. We returned from college and found his room locked. In fact,

About a Chair

it was just yesterday that we found out that his father is not keeping well.'

Later that evening, as Vivi sat out in the balcony, she dreamt out aloud about how life would stir with discontent if Clement for some reason never came back again, letting her be all alone on the balcony while the beauty of the night was lost on two yearning eyes. She knew it was selfish to wish for someone who was away honouring his duty as a faithful son, but the long days had left her longing for the comfort of his silent company.

◆

Thud. Thud. The heavy impact of a busy hammer.

The noise woke Vivi up. She looked at the clock on the table—ten past six—and lifted the curtain on the window to check where the noise was coming from. It was Clement on his balcony, hammering away at the old chair. He paused every now and then to rock it and check its sturdiness. The creaking of the chair, after a couple of nails into its joints, was reduced to a muffled squeal.

Vivi got off her bed, walked out to the balcony, and stood there awkwardly for him to take notice. Some time passed with him absorbed in his work, then he quickly looked at her way and timidly smiled. Vivi acknowledged his effort by smiling back. He went back to hammering without skipping a beat.

After he was done, he got up and turned her way with a strange expression on his face, as if he was at the precipice

A Kite of Farewells

of saying something important. She noticed his mouth part slightly, a word about to roll off from the tip of his tongue, only to eventually give in to hesitation. A quick nod was all he could muster before he disappeared into his room.

That evening she saw him again on the balcony, this time uneasy with his own company, letting out loud sighs between the puffs of his cigarette. The chair squealed when he pushed himself forward on it, which clearly bothered him.

When night approached, he got up slowly and dragged the chair back into his room. Then, the light in his room went off a little earlier than usual.

◆

It was about ten minutes past six the next morning when Vivi was awoken by the piercing siren of an ambulance and the frantic knocking on the door of her room. On opening the door, she was met with the ghostly face of Toli, who did not waste a minute in telling her:

'That guy, Clement, h-he hung himself last night.' She shook as she said those words.

'What do you mean he hung himself? I just saw him yesterday on the balcony repairing his chair.' Vivi wished at that moment with every ounce of her being that she was still dreaming.

But in the span of the few hours between the ambulance leaving with Clement's body and the whole neighbourhood gathering around the apartment, she grew to accept the cruel reality of his suicide.

About a Chair

In the evening, Vivi, Toli, Toli's boyfriend and their friends all gathered on the balcony wearing a certain look of sadness and bartered stories about Clement, or whatever they had heard of him from others. It came to the fore after a while that he had been depressed for some time. The depression got more serious with the news of his father's sickness, which turned out to be terminal cancer.

'Maybe all this time he had been screaming out for help—you know, the whole creaking of the chair thing,' Toli said between deep sighs.

Vivi wondered what could have happened if she had stayed a little longer on the balcony that fateful evening when he was hammering the chair. Or maybe, just maybe, if he had not hesitated and spoken those words. The same words that would forever be left unspoken now.

◆

Months passed after that incident, but Vivi couldn't bring herself to sit on the balcony again without thinking of Clement and his chair. The balcony looked barren with creepers coiled around the railings, and the 'To Let' banner collecting dust added to the desolation.

On her last day in Guwahati and her last evening in the apartment, she summoned all the courage in her reserve and walked to the balcony to take in the sight of the opposite balcony for the final time. A kurta and pyjama drying on the railing told of a recent occupant. The old chair had also been brought out on the balcony and was sporting new upholstery.

A Kite of Farewells

She sat down on a chair in the balcony under the mellow evening sun, and let her mind wander to the past. Lost in the thoughts of that stranger on the balcony, she was overwhelmed with sadness. But after the sadness there was gratitude—gratitude for the feeling of being comforted with his silent company when her world was coming apart at the seams.

She noticed tears welling up in her eyes. She had not cried since her father's scandal, not a drop when her father smacked her for the first time, not when she ran away from home because she couldn't take it any longer, not when her first boyfriend dumped her because she was poor, and not even when the news of the suicide found her ear early in the morning.

With tears rolling down her cheeks, she whispered, 'I hear you now, Clement.'

Code Blue

'How much for two tickets?' I asked the guy at the counter.

From behind the counter, a small compartment made of plywood with a head-sized cut-out facing the entrance, the guy leaned forward to have a close look at me. I had every reason to not be there—this was no place for kids. I was fourteen with the face of a thirteen-year-old, with my school uniform stuffed inside my bag and a nervy best friend on the lookout behind me.

◆

It was the early 2000s, and this small town in the lap of mist-topped mountains was warming up to the optimism of the new millennium, as it offered in its epochal strides all the latest modern conveniences for a steal. First, it was the cheap portable radios that families would huddle around in the evening as the teeny-weeny voice inside them regaled them with programmes that covered everything from local news

A Kite of Farewells

to cloying hair metal ballads. Then the television arrived, furthering the collective hunger for imported escapism: bootleg Hollywood blockbusters and skin flicks (popularly known as blue films) came to hypnotize the masses, fuelling the booming pirated CD rental business coming up around every corner, which replaced the sleepy VCR rental shops from the last decade.

It was not before long when someone had an epiphany and decided to open a cinema hall—calling it a cinema hall would be far too generous, for it was just a stuffy room with wooden benches for sitting—close to the dingy shops selling cheap alcohol, a degenerate institution for the colony drunks to let loose their intoxicated shenanigans before fumbling back home under the flickering street lamps.

After school, on my walk back, I would pass through that side of town. On mouldy plywood boards, the posters of the day's screening were tacked on: the morning shows were the usual kung fu movies with preposterous titles, while in the evening it would mostly be skin flicks. As I would slowly walk past the roaring commotion of wild applause and peals of laughter behind the closed door of these cinema halls, I would get an eyeful of the large, lurid posters with naked ladies on the show boards. To be honest, a part of me wanted to be in their company, partaking in their sinful voyeurism.

◆

'Do you know I saw a fight there yesterday?' I nudged Wilson, who was busy with his scrapbook.

'Tell me about it.' Wilson looked up.

'Well, I saw two guys enacting kung fu moves at each other. It looked fun until one guy bloodied the nose of the other. I left quickly when things got heated.'

Wilson, for some reason, was drawn to outlandish stories, and I did not lack in that department.

After gleefully listening to the day's quota of such stories, Wilson leaned forward and asked in a whisper:

'So, when is the Big Day Out?'

The Big Day Out, as we called it, had been our conversation centrepiece for the past few days. We had been planning to bunk a day of classes and do something radical before the year-end—a clear result of compulsive reading of *The Hardy Boys*. We were still figuring out what exactly qualified as 'truly radical'.

During one of the many brainstorming sessions at lunch, Wilson had blurted out, 'What about watching a blue film together inside those cinema halls?'

'That's,' I searched for the proper word, 'awesome!'

'But they don't—'

'Allow school kids inside,' I completed his sentence.

The last time I remembered watching a blue film with some company was at a senior's place when his parents were away for some work in Kohima. The curtains were drawn shut and the lights switched off as the colony boys, huddled inside the common room, spoke in whispers. However, the low-volume experience, as dictated by the circumstance, was interrupted every now and then by freezing of the frame,

A Kite of Farewells

which the host took care of by ejecting the CD and blowing his breath onto it—it somehow worked every time.

'What about the last day of sports week?' I asked Wilson. 'There will be no roll call and we can carry casuals inside our bags to change into later. We will wait in the bush for some time and slip away.'

The 'bush'—an abandoned construction plot surrounded by dense thickets and a favourite hideout among class bunkers. It was littered with chips packets, rolled-up glue tubes and discoloured hankies, telling of its close association with the school delinquents—the glue sniffers. A month ago, there was a rumour going around about a wild cat lurking in the 'bush'. The students were clever enough to brush it it off as yet another attempt by the school authorities to discourage students from bunking.

'Are you sure about it?' Wilson asked sternly.

'Damn sure,' I replied.

◆

The following Thursday, we met at the 'bush', casuals and chips in our bags, waiting for the loudspeakers to come on. The morning announcement would mean the day's programme was on and we could slip away without being noticed.

'Want some chips?' Wilson produced a packet from his bag, and added, 'I don't feel good about this whole thing.'

'Listen, we agreed to do this together, so man the hell up.' I was this close to shouting.

Code Blue

The last thing I wanted was to be abandoned to the buzzing of mosquitoes for the whole day in the 'bush'. Every minute wasted on indecision increased our chances of being caught.

I snatched the packet of chips and stuffed my mouth with all the chips I could grab.

'Hey, leave something for me too,' protested Wilson.

I shrugged at him—that's the price for doubting our well-oiled plan.

'Okay, okay. We are doing this.' He punched the air.

Just as we got up to leave, a dry rustling of leaves crept upon us from behind. Wilson, being the apprehensive kid, stood to an electric attention.

'It's the wild cat,' he remarked.

'Shut up, will you!' I tiptoed towards the bush and slowly parted it to the sides to steal a view.

In a near circle was another group of bunkers hunched over with polythene bags in their hands, huffing glue. It looked like quite a struggle for them to keep their bloodied eyes open for even a minute. I didn't want to risk attracting unnecessary attention to us, so I turned back to Wilson and assured him:

'It's those glue sniffers. Let's change and leave.'

I undid my necktie, threw it inside the bag and got my jacket out. This faded brown jacket was a Christmas gift from Shillong. I hated—and still hate—its sterile design, but that morning it was the only jacket not inside the laundry basket. The whiff of its musky smell never failed to bring

A Kite of Farewells

to mind an old neighbour who only got out of his house to make the monthly routine trip to his posting in Tuensang to withdraw his salary. On other days of the month, he loitered around his barricaded garden that barely grew anything to merit his labour.

◆

'How many tickets?' asked the guy behind the counter. He had a certain look about him, like one of those school dropouts with spiked hair (punk hair as we called it), and spoke in crude slangs.

'Two,' I replied.

He dragged forward his plastic chair to take a better look at my face—he looked unamused.

'Just a minute,' he disappeared into the room behind the counter, and was heard noisily pushing the furniture over the wooden floor, presumably looking for something.

'He suspects us. We should run before it's too late,' said Wilson, his face red with panic.

I gestured at him to be silent.

The guy slipped back into the counter with a half-pint whisky bottle and a porcelain-white pannikin cup. He threw himself down on the chair with force and poured the whisky into the cup.

'Just a minute,' he reached down, got out a bottle of mineral water, and then proceeded to pour it into the cup with the precision and attention of an experienced surgeon.

After enduring the hot breath of foul-smelling alcohol

on my face, I was handed two pieces of paper with the word 'ticket' written on it in shaky cursive.

'That will be twenty rupees.'

We were set for the adventure to come.

We seated ourselves at the back, far from any scrutiny. The air inside was stuffy and heavily smelt of the fetid alcohol from earlier. The limbs of the occupants, most of them drunk, were lazily hanging over the wooden benches in a waggish display of inconceivable geometry.

The door closed and the lights went off—it was met with a round of applause.

The next forty minutes to follow were the quickest forty minutes of my life. What lay bare on the projected screen did not compare to the joy of participating in the collective antics of the audience. 'Get to the action,' yelled someone from the front row when we were five minutes in—the audience clapped wildly and cheered. Besides the obvious, there wasn't anything interesting in the plot. I turned towards Wilson, seated behind me, who was busy cheering along with the audience; I noticed his legs were firmly crossed.

'This is actually fun,' said Wilson, his eyes fixed on the screen. 'Not the film, but—'

'The audience,' I concurred.

♦

Six years after college graduation, I stood at the school gate flooded with nostalgia. I had always prided myself as someone unaffected by memories. But that day, a breezy July evening,

A Kite of Farewells

as the sun was dipping low into Mount Tiyi, I had this sudden and inexplicable urge to drop by this old haunt of mine. The walls had thick patches of moss, the classrooms looked revamped and had state-of-the-art smart boards (back then, having LED monitors in the computer lab qualified as cutting edge), the chairs were now engineered wood units, the basketball court, freshly painted, had brand new hoops, and a new building was coming up with workers levelling the concrete mix with trowels as they scaled up and down the bamboo scaffolding with ease.

When I got back home, I got busy rummaging through the bookshelf in the hope of finding something from my school days.

I came upon a familiar old notebook with a lozenge-shaped sticker on its cover. Written on it were the words *'Property of Master Wilson'*—Wilson's beloved scrapbook.

I had no idea how it had ended up there. It would take the might of the whole world to wrestle it away from his grip back in school. This was one of the few things that was unconditionally dear to him.

As I flipped through the pages, now yellow with age, I landed on a page with a piece of paper neatly taped to its right corner: a hurriedly torn piece with the word 'ticket' written on it in poor handwriting. Just below it, he had written in a boyish handwriting:

Code Blue

Best day of my life.
Best friends forever.

A warm, wholesome feeling of completeness coursed through my body. I let out a childish chuckle.

My mind raced back to that day—the day when two pubescent boys walked out of a cinema hall into the world of men.

Flower in the Wild

I WAS SIX YEARS OLD THEN, but I figured something was off from the way a sombre hush suddenly descended upon the modest name-giving party of about forty people.

◆

It was the christening party of the newest member of our growing family—my baby sister, born in the early hours of a June Sunday with the monsoon rain banging on the tin roof of our wattle-and-daub government quarter. With the yellow tinge of the morning sun glazing the frosty window panels, I remember waking up to the sound of hurried footsteps outside the room where I slept with my younger brother. I pushed myself out of the bed, my eyes half open, and kicked around to find my chappals. An uncle passing through the room saw me awake and called out to me:

'Ngongo, up already? Good, come with me, quick.'

I slipped into my oversized chappals and shuffled along.

'What happened?' I asked.

Flower in the Wild

'You will know soon,' he remarked gleefully.

When I made my way into the room, I saw Mother on the bed, cradling a sleeping baby in her tired arms.

'Look, it's your sister,' said my uncle, nudging me forward. 'Go on, have a look.'

She was swaddled in a polka-dot blanket with only her tiny face and gloved hands showing through. A part of me wanted to pinch her plump cheeks, not to give in to an impish impulse but to ascertain that she—my baby sister—was indeed flesh and bones and not one of those lifelike plastic dolls they have up in the storefronts in Police Point, the main town in Wokha.

When I leaned forward, I saw the most beautiful pair of eyes looking back at me with wonder. In that moment, even my child self knew that she was going to be the most precious person in the house.

I held her tiny hands in mine until she fell asleep, still clutching my finger. I gently ran my fingers over her sleeping face—she responded by twitching her mouth.

◆

In the kitchen, as I was sipping on the morning jaha, my younger brother rushed in with his toothbrush still in his froth-filled mouth.

'Ata, Ata,' he called out in excitement. 'Have you seen the baby? Have you seen our kaka?'

I responded in affirmation.

The last time he had seemed that excited about anything

A Kite of Farewells

was the day Father took him down to town on his second-hand Yamaha RX bike to buy him a certain toy he had been raving about for days. The toy in question—a battery-operated Jeep model. It went everywhere with him, leaving tiny tyre marks in his imaginary open road. I figured it would not last a month given the shoddy build of the toy, but to my surprise, that cheap mould of plastic and cranky tyres held their own for a good year. Eventually he got bored of it and traded it with an older kid next door for a comic book. It was to be noted that he wasn't yet able to comprehend written words that well, but every night after he was done with his homework, he would splash down on the bed beside me and guide me through the colourful panels of the comic while putting up a commendable effort to read aloud the sentences inside the speech bubbles. I would interrupt at times to point out certain dialogues that evaded even my comprehension, and proceed to make up the most ridiculous story on the spot. He would listen with rapt attention to my cock-and-bull story. But upon realizing that I was just making things up, he would grumpily stuff the comic book under his pillow and go to sleep without a word.

◆

'Ngongo, take your brother and go to the kitchen,' my aunt said.

I was dressed in a tailored waistcoat and even wore my favourite Bata shoes polished to a shine, sitting on one of the benches arranged in rows under a makeshift tarpaulin tent.

Flower in the Wild

In my hand I held a folded copy of the invitation, which was plain given the financial situation—Father was running helter-skelter looking for any job to keep the lights on in the house.

Pots of steaming rice and pork cooked in bamboo shoots, and plates of hotchpotch salad and crispy brown papads came flying out of the kitchen in the hands of the colony women folks who had been up the previous night, toiling and chattering into the late hours.

I heard all of them sigh with relief as they laid the pots on the teak dining table outside, right next to the stacks of cheap plastic plates and disposable cups, and a plate of ripe bananas.

But I figured that something had gone awry by the way the pervasive atmosphere of gaiety abruptly made way for a deafening hush. I noticed the sudden traffic of alarmed faces rushing into the room where Mother was with Kaka. I got up and disappeared into the rush to make sense of what was going on.

I tapped on the shoulder of one of my aunts standing outside the door.

'Ano, what happened? Why is everyone going inside?' I asked.

Her hand reached around my shoulder, enveloping me in her gloomy silence. A faint sobbing was heard through the thin walls. It sounded like Mother, but it was hard to tell, especially given the agitated fluttering of the tarpaulin sheet outside that had been shaken into activity by the wind coming in from the west.

A Kite of Farewells

Father walked out tailed by two of my uncles, but before I could ask him anything, Ano signalled to the colony aunties to usher me and my brother to the kitchen.

'Something happened to Kaka, na?' my brother asked.

One of the colony aunties quickly looked to the corner at one of her companions, telling so much yet so little with her woeful eyes.

'Something is wrong with Ayo, na?' my brother continued.

'Shhh, Ngongo,' the lady commented. 'I will tell you everything after you are finished with the tea I am making for both of you.'

Tea was soon served in oversized pannikin cups with a bowl of rusk biscuits. We noisily munched on the biscuit, sipping the tea in brisk intervals; the lady sat down on a moora beside us. Her eyes were stirring with pity at our naivety.

'Your Kaka…' She paused.

I craned my neck out the window to the loud outburst of crying outside. I saw Ayo inconsolable, with a still Kaka in her arms. I got up and pressed my person against the latched door, and watched them get into a car and disappear into the thick blanket of dust the road threw up behind its track.

'…is with God now.'

♦

In the boredom of waiting, I got out the folded invitation card inside my pocket, laid it out flat on the moora, and read it aloud:

Flower in the Wild

You are cordially invited to the christening ceremony of our beloved daughter Meriyani…

Our sister, Kaka Meriyani, passed away on her christening day into the world of dreams.

◆

That night, the womenfolk got busy packing all the food into milk-powder packets and newspaper sheets. Every guest left with a packet or two in their hands. The plates stacked on the table were left untouched. Cups of tea kept flying out from the kitchen to the people huddled around a small bonfire; they were engrossed in a conversation of frugal words and deep collective sighs.

◆

Twenty years came to pass. We had moved to a new address where we welcomed two more boys into the family, the boys now in their early teenage years. It was the second week of December and I was soaking in the early morning sun of Wokha while silently counting the days to go before I moved back to the city for my studies. The family was taking cognizance of the activities planned for the month with cups of tea in hand. Soon, chatter grew among us, covering everything from the sheer number of wedding cards reaching our house to how they don't make songs like 'Choro Kupi' anymore.

'There are two weddings happening at the same time tomorrow. We should decide who will attend which wedding,' said Father humorously.

A Kite of Farewells

In the spirit of wedding jest, Mother mentioned an incident when we were in primary school and attending our first big fat Naga wedding—a distant cousin's. We had tasted custard for the first time and liked it so much that we ate a dozen from the serving table in quick succession. The other guests had not been amused.

'Oh, talking about childhood memories, do you remember that comic book I used to have, the one I used to keep under the pillow?' asked my brother.

The other two brothers were clueless about what he was talking about.

'Yes, I do. What about that?' I asked.

'Nothing, just remembered it,' he paused. 'I never saw it again after that day.'

'What day?' I asked.

'The day Kaka passed away,' he replied.

After a moment of silence, Ayo chipped in:

'Someone might have mistakenly used it to wrap food items. There were plenty of leftovers that day. There were so many—'

'Ayo, that day when you left with Kaka in the car, leaving us in the kitchen, where did you go to bury her?' I interrupted.

Ayo looked at me, sighed loudly, and said:

'If my memory serves me right, it was a stone's throw away from Nimotsu's grave. Given the sudden nature of her demise, we had to make do with a last-minute grave. One of your uncles had a coffin made by a carpenter living next door, and the carpenter was kind enough to make us a crude crucifix from the spare wood lying around.'

I had been to Amotsu's grave two years ago on his death anniversary with a bouquet of flowers. It was in the centre of the public cemetery, below the Assam Rifles camp. From Amotsu's grave, scores of crucifixes—cement and wooden ones—with names forgotten to those living, spread out radially right up to the fence, on the other side of which thick bushes grew profusely. In the eerie silence of the place, one is reminded that death is indeed the ultimate equalizer.

♦

The next day, with the evening sun steadily slipping down the rugged contour of Mount Tiyi, the family stood over a small hump of soil with a musty crucifix planted on it. Thick shrubs had overrun the area, some even reaching up to the knee; the caretaker of the cemetery could only be seen on pay day, and his whereabouts were a mystery to many, including the dead.

'The words on the crucifix have faded,' said Mother as she laid a bouquet of flowers against the crucifix.

I kneeled, pressed my hand against the crucifix, and wiped off the dust till the indentations of the engraving were visible:

RIP
Our beloved daughter,
Meriyani Lotha,
Who passed away on the day
she got a name.

Time

THE ROAR OF THUNDER SHOT through the slumbering sky, after jagged bolts of lightning hurled down into the mountains as the heavens emptied themselves.

And of all the days in a week, I forgot to bring an umbrella that day. It was evident, judging by the morning's thick blanket of grey clouds hovering above the buildings, that monsoon was here, and it would not be kind to anyone with a to-do list for the day.

Under the awning of a café, I stretched my hand out to gauge the intensity of the downpour. The café was new with extra-large, glass-panelled windows. 'Café Scooter' read the sign above the door in flowery calligraphy, alongside a small cut-out of a yellow Bajaj scooter. From the sound of rumbling conversations coming from inside, it was packed—not unusual for a café on a Friday afternoon in this part of the town. Café culture was a recent cultural import. In fact, a year ago, there were only two cafés in the whole town; now, every corner has at least one tucked between old buildings. Even the rice hotels from yesteryears—most of them conveniently located near highways—which made good money from serving hungry travellers plates of warm rice and pork, jumped on the bandwagon and rebranded themselves as 'rice café' (the menu remained unchanged though). This is a trend-obsessed town, and it pays to follow it. Seated on white bar stools with garish fanny bags slung across their shoulders, a clique of college students with hip haircuts looked at me from the balcony of another new café across the road. Out of a sense of insecurity, I looked down at my old sneakers—they weren't that terribly out of fashion.

I stood there for some time and watched the rain sweep over the overbridges and the street lights, and against defiant umbrellas pushing through the barrage of silvery raindrops. The seductive aroma of the coffee brewing inside the cafés diffused into the footpath, making me want to call off the day and waste the hours with a cup of coffee. But it was too early for coffee, and I had places to be.

I pulled back the sleeve of my jacket and looked at my watch—10.45.

The hands seemed to be frozen, so I tapped on it gently, then persuasively; the waterproof material must have given out because it did nothing.

So my watch became another addition to the day's growing list of disappointments.

About the watch, nothing remarkable about it, but I was quite fond of it. It was a gift from my ex-girlfriend,

A Kite of Farewells

who said a lot of unsavoury things when angry but knew how to give a gift. The watch looked like it was made for my sinewy hand. It had been with me for three years, and except for the brown leather strap that needed replacing once, it ticked as good as new.

I got my phone out and switched it on—11.28.

I was officially late for my appointment. The idea of wasting the day inside one of the cafés seemed enticing. But one quick look at the watch again, and I resolved to get at least one thing done before the end of the day.

Two shops ahead of me, a wooden board with the words 'Nini's Repair Shop' jutted out into the footpath.

An old man, in his late fifties, with thick prescription glasses perched on his nose bridge, sat on a stool, resting his heavy arms on the table, his eyes fixed on the people outside, dashing from one end to another. His eyes, brown and beady, glistened with melancholy, and the steam from the cup of tea placed in front of him added to the dramatic aesthetic of the sight. I stood at an arm's length from the shop, uncertain if I should steal him away from his moment of leisure.

'Uncle,' I asked, 'do you repair wristwatches here?'

'Oh, I am sorry, I didn't notice you,' he turned towards me. 'Yes, watch repairing, TV repairing, all repairing done here.'

'I have this watch of mine to fix.' I produced the watch still strapped to my hand.

'You need to take it off first, young man,' he said with an amused smile.

I obliged with an awkward nod.

Time

'And for the love of God and everything wet in this wretched weather, come inside and have a seat,' he continued.

I followed again by grabbing one of the two stools inside and flopping down on it, to quite my relief.

'Perhaps a cup of ginger tea too?' he pointed to the chrome flask sitting on the table. I politely refused, not wanting to burden him too much.

'Let's see what this one is up to,' he hunched over a small, untidy desk riddled with tools and mechanical parts of varied forms and sizes, lit by a single CFL bulb dangling from the ceiling. The wall right in front of the desk was adorned with a chaotic array of wall clocks, old and repaired ones, ticking in loud lags that became even more discernible on closer inspection.

'You know,' the man turned towards me, 'in this business of repairs these days, it's usually the old folks coming in for repairs and quick fixes. Young customers are a rarity.'

'I guess old people know how to treasure their possessions,' I replied, further adding, 'but if I may ask, Uncle, if business is not good like the way it used to be, then what motivates you to keep the shop open?' No sooner had I said these words did I realize how impolite I sounded, especially considering how nice he had been.

'I am sorry that was—' I quickly followed it up but was interrupted.

'It's okay, young man. I don't mind answering your question, but it is a long story, something you'd have to sit through for hours maybe.'

A Kite of Farewells

The patterning of the rain was growing in ferocity outside, and the water from the drains was flowing onto the footpath, making a messy situation for the pedestrians. It was apparent that the rain had no intention of subsiding in the next two or three hours. So I figured that I'd much rather be richer by a story by the time the rain stops.

'Uncle, the offer for the ginger tea still stands?' I asked.

He laughed aloud and poured me a cup from the flask. I held the hot, disposable paper cup in my cold hands and brought it to my face to feel the warm ginger-scented steam coming off it. The feeling of it reminded me of the nights at the college canteen when I used to correct answer sheets while gulping down cups of ginger tea. Since those days, I have come to associate ginger tea with labour. But that day, by some weird magic of the rain outside, I enjoyed drinking it.

'Would you like some biscuits too?' he offered me a packet of Parle-G, which I politely refused.

'Why don't you tell me a little about yourself first? I don't entertain guests that often in my shop,' he asked.

'Well, I...' I paused to collect my thoughts, 'am Miko. I am a teacher, recently appointed. I have just moved into my first-ever apartment in Minister Hill, which right now is just a bed, a table and a chair. But hey, I don't have to buy water as the compound has a community well.'

My phone in the pocket of my jeans lit up, hijacking my train of thoughts with the incessant warbling of birds in the wilderness—I have a proclivity for setting nature sounds as my ringtone. The caller name on the screen read 'Mom'— I unhesitatingly rejected the call.

'Today, I had a job interview that I missed because I forgot my umbrella and my watch—' The warbling of the birds commenced again, cutting me off.

Mom again—I pressed decline, switched off the phone, and slipped it back into my pocket. No more interruptions.

'Are you going to answer that?' he asked.

'It's not important right now,' I told him and forced a smile at half-mast.

◆

Would you possibly blame everything wrong in your life on a single person, especially when that person is your own mother? Even the death of the only person who truly understood you—your father—something you have not fully recovered from. Well, I do, vehemently and with a reason. My mother is, without contest, unconventional and, most times, a difficult person. Maybe it was how she was raised—in a big house with an absentee military father—that hardened her from the inside and made her cold and distant, suspicious of every affection, and an absolute control freak. Maybe it was the simmering resentment building up in intensity for all the lost years of a supposed carefree youth forgone for a hasty decision one fateful November evening when she and father got hitched, abandoning her easy life in the city to settle in a nondescript small town—they were both in their early twenties when they got married. When I look back at

A Kite of Farewells

the years growing up, I feel like a puppet strung up for the entertainment of an audience of one—the puppeteer, my mother. From things like the way I dress to hard choices like my career, she had a say in every decision of my life. Much of my childhood, or I dare say my entire life, has been one big, uneventful blur. A blur of non-events. But all of this wouldn't matter much if not for the fact that she had been a lousy wife too; she was frugal in her affection towards Father, even when he was dying.

'Shall I start my story now?' he asked.

I gestured at him to begin.

'I opened this shop in 2005, but I had been entertaining the idea of it for a long time. Before this shop, I used to be a guy with a good government job and a beautiful family. I had a wife and a daughter. I was literally living the Naga Dream.'

'Government job?' I asked.

'Yes, I was working in the Secretariat, which then was a new building with too many empty rooms.'

'Anyway,' he continued, 'for the first few years in service, I was doing everything up to standard, sometimes even going above and beyond the call of duty to impress my superiors. The perks and privileges that came with the office were endless. But soon, boredom crept in—work became monotonous and unchallenging. I badly wanted to feel the thrill of being young again and not knowing what the day would throw at me. That boredom eventually found its way into the house. The love I felt from my wife and daughter gradually became not enough. So where did I go to feel alive again? Among the company of chronic alcoholics in the same office.

'A peg, and another peg, and suddenly everything around me sprang to life in an alluring dance of pure jest. A few weeks with my new company, I became a regular sight in all the slummy, sleazy motu ghors—much to the delight of the owners, mostly voluptuous jolly spinsters with rosy cheeks and perky bosoms. A flirty exchange here and there with the owners was a given when the booze-fuelled game of cards went on till the sleepy hours past midnight.

'In the midst of all my antics, back at home, my wife would wait for me through the night, with cold plates set out on the dining table. Early in the morning, when I would find my way back home, looking miserable and with a foul temper, she would attend to me without uttering a word. I dare say that the way she didn't protest my drunken antics emboldened my foolishness even more. There were times when I went missing from the house for days only to be found sleeping on a bench in one of the motu ghors.

'My wife was a graceful woman, a generous soul, something I took full advantage of.'

'I am sorry, but if I may ask, how did you meet her?' I enquired.

'We were college sweethearts,' he replied and continued, 'I married her a year after graduation. Alright, back to the story. Some years after I joined the office, the night before the day our daughter was born, I walked into the delivery room with the morning sun peeking through the curtains, dragging my feet over the tiled corridor of the hospital, and smelling of whisky from the previous night—yes, I was away, drinking into the late hours the night before my daughter was born.

'What was to be the punishment for such a vice? There was none. As expected, my wife didn't say a word, but she clearly looked disappointed at me. But even in my hungover condition, the moment I held my daughter—tiny, tender and pure—all of her in my palms, I felt a growing warmth inside me, the kind that had evaded me for a long time. My world, endless and confusing, started to shrink till it was just the four corners of the hospital room—with me, my wife and my beloved daughter in it. A feeling of determination took over me—a God-given duty to protect this world of mine from the evils of the world. But my new state of sobriety didn't last for long, as old habits soon came knocking without invitation.

'With our daughter growing older, the once-docile nature of my wife was traded for a befitting assertiveness, much to the dismay of my drinking peers, and welcomed with hostility from my end. She did not want our daughter's life to be yet another bet in my gamble. Silent as she might have been before, she was now determined to clean my act up and steer me away from the intoxicating seduction of the booze towards the tepid calling of responsible parenting.

'"The absolute guts of that woman!" I'd cursed. On nights when I dragged into the house all the bad blood from the gambling table, the same guts got my temper flaring and fists flying, landing heavily on her frail frame—with my daughter looking in through the door left ajar, terrified of the monster at home.

'She watched passively through the cracks of her crumbling world, cowering under the bleak shadow cast by the angry man in the house. It hardened her from the inside, taught her to be stiff and cold to affection. I was still too consumed in my vices to notice her silent resentment grow with each passing day. By the time she was old enough to leave for college, we were pretty much estranged—barely seeing eye to eye on anything. I would noisily object to the things that I felt she did deliberately to annoy me, which was a long list, and she would fire back with the same. She definitely shared my stubbornness.

'On the last day of her vacation, after which she was to report back to her hostel in Dimapur, she walked into the study room and asked if I could drop her off the next day to her hostel. I was already three pegs down in my evening round of Chivas Regal, and seething with indignation at the current state of affairs in the house, so without even looking her way, I refused. It was to be the costliest mistake of my life. The next day, without a goodbye, she took an early morning taxi and left before the sun came up. Her mother saw her off at the taxi stand with packets of home-cooked food.

'Sometime after lunch, in the late evening, I got a call from my brother. I could make out the distress in his voice.

A Kite of Farewells

With conspicuous pauses he informed me:

"'Your daughter... The taxi she was in met with an accident near Patkai Bridge. I am on my way to the site... I will update when I reach there."

'My heart sank to the floor. I had my fair share of commuting by local taxis in my younger days, and the phrase "safe local taxi" is a misleading oxymoron, with mostly alcoholics and no-good high-school dropouts behind the steering wheel, manoeuvring rusty Tata Sumos through steep, winding terrains with what little volition is left with them after the drinks. To exacerbate the situation, these taxis would often be loaded with excess luggage from local businesses looking to save a few bucks by dumping their goods on the roof of the taxis. The taxi my daughter got into that morning was no exception, with an inebriated driver, a year or two older than herself, excess luggage overhead, and passengers packed shoulder to shoulder. While negotiating a particularly notorious U-turn, near the infamous Patkai Bridge, the left rear tyre, wobbling under the excess weight, gave away, leading to the taxi skidding over the wet shoulder of the road and down into the gorge, rolling over the protruding rocks and wiry trees until it was completely wrecked and almost in halves.

'My daughter—seated in the middle seat—and the seven other passengers were killed on the spot, with only the driver found feebly breathing when help arrived. He was hospitalized in the ICU; after a week-long coma, he too breathed his last. Looking back now, I wish I had set aside my ego that fateful evening at the study table and agreed to drive her to her hostel. My precious baby would have been still alive. I don't care if she would have continued to loathe the sight of me with passion, but she would be alive.'

With tears in his eyes, he looked into the distance.

'It still eats me every night.'

'I am so sorry for your loss, Uncle,' I offered my condolences.

'The evening following the funeral programme, I came back to this thick air of gloom permeating every inch and corner of the house, and then I noticed something come over my wife like a shadow. From that day, she became numb, devoid of any signs of life. She went around the house like a tree stripped bare or a river left parched by the scorching sun. It did not take a genius to infer that I was the cause of this development. In the eyes of the woman who did not utter a word while braving my drunken shenanigans through the years, I saw for the first time an acute look of disdain.

'After my daughter's passing, I didn't drink even a drop for a month, but I am a man who is easily bored, and by the next month, I found my way back to the motu ghors, this time drinking away my sorrows. Even the owners were concerned at the rate at which I was gulping down pegs after pegs.

'I was getting old too, and the drinking soon caught up with me: it started with searing pain in my abdomen, which made even walking impossible. Then followed the vomiting, sometimes with traces of blood. I knew it was time to pay

A Kite of Farewells

the dues for all the reckless years of defiling my body with alcohol.

'After a surgery that nearly bankrupted us, I was able to get back on track to a renewed life of sobriety and much-needed pondering. I still needed assistance to go about my daily business post surgery; my wife shadowed me day and night, right from the bedroom to the toilet. When I rested in the evening, she would disappear into our daughter's room with a broom in hand, cleaning and arranging it the way she left it that day, and come out after an hour with swollen eyes. Late one evening, braving the pain in my legs, I dragged myself into the same room, staring at the festoon of photographs, of her and her friends, hung on the wall beside the window. I sat down on the bed, blankets neatly folded with clean pillows, and looked around through the tears in my eyes. I braced myself and cried my heart out—for all the times I had taken the people around me for granted.

'As the dying light outside the window made way for the night, I turned to the clock on the wall, an old Ajanta clock with a chrome pendulum. Its hands were frozen in time—so much like the room and the people who frequented it. I took it down to my makeshift workshop at the back of the kitchen and spent the whole night taking it apart piece by piece. By next day noon, after obsessively tinkering with it, I had a fair understanding of its intricate mechanism. In the ensuing months, as I recovered in strength and resolve, I took on this new obsession of repairing and improving anything and everything I could get my hands on: the kitchen drawer saw a new coat of paint along with new hinges, the creaky chair on the verandah got a new frame, the water tanks got cleaned and their leaks sealed, the TV remote buttons were cooperating for the first time.

'But watches and clocks fascinated me like no other. I was collecting old watches from friends and neighbours and taking them apart, religiously studying their delicate parts under the dim light of the workshop, sometimes even forgoing my dinner.

'One December evening, after a busy day of decorating the house for Christmas Day, I stole my wife away from her evening routine of reading near the fireplace to the front of the house. While she waited unenthused by my new-found cheer, I dramatically flicked the switch on—the house came alive with the flickering hues of the decorative Christmas lights. She stood still, devoid of emotions, then turned to walk back into the house with her hands tucked inside her cardigan. That Christmas, our house sported the brightest yet loneliest decorations in the whole colony. My wife's words were becoming bare like her enthusiasm for life. She merely existed, hollow from the inside, looking out into the world, waiting for the day to turn into night, and seasons into years. I noticed that she was ageing faster too.

'My makeshift workshop soon got an upgrade, becoming a full-fledged one filled with eye loupes, cleaning kits, soldering tools, and of course rows of repaired clocks on the walls. My wife came in one morning with my breakfast,

A Kite of Farewells

sat on the stool, and watched me repair a neighbour's wristwatch; when I got it back to ticking like brand new, I waved it at my wife with the enthusiasm of a child who had just won a lottery—she smiled for the first time and told me, "You are surrounded by all these clocks, yet the irony is that you were reckless with the one thing when it mattered the most: your time." The weight of those words still haunts me to this date.

'On 27th June 2003, my wife passed away after having been bed-ridden from a prolonged illness, leaving me alone to wander the empty rooms of the house, sometimes late at night, in bouts of panic at the realization of the overbearing grief that had enveloped my life. During the day, I drifted from room to room—mostly my daughter's room and the master bedroom—cleaning and arranging every object inside them till they showed some semblance of active ownership. In the evening, I disappeared into my workshop to work on old and broken watches till the late hours. A year later, I took voluntary retirement to much protest from my relatives.

'It did not take me long before the whimsical thought of opening a repair shop in the town became more than just a thought—I had a modest amount saved up in my account—and by the winter of 2005, I had this room leased to me. On the first day of business, I entertained my first batch of customers, mostly former colleagues from the office who dropped in out of curiosity and not so much out of necessity. They all thought that I had lost my mind to be doing such a petty thing. After the talk in the town about the mad man who had resigned from government service to open a watch repair shop petered out, people started flocking to my shop for repairs. Word got around that the mad man was indeed great with repairs. Absorbed in the details of the repairs, hunched over the table, I did not notice time slipping by outside my shop. But during lunch—the same fried rice with omelette—when I let my eyes wander into the distance, I noticed new buildings come up the corner and new showrooms open and close, sometimes within the same month. The world was changing regardless of whether I noticed it or not. It was marching onward, and I was getting too old to keep up.

'So your earlier question, young man,' he leaned forward, "what motivates me to keep the shop open in spite of low footfall these days?"

'I do it for my daughter.

'My wife was not wrong when she told me I had no time for the people when it mattered the most. Also, among these old and repaired stuffs, broken but still ticking, I feel right at home.'

'I see,' I said. 'Thank you for sharing your story with me. And I am so sorry about your daughter and your wife.'

'Don't be. I don't get this opportunity that often. And here—' He got up and handed me my watch. While narrating his story, his deft hands had been working on the watch, making it work like nothing had happened.

'It was a minor battery issue,' he informed me.

A Kite of Farewells

I strapped it back on and looked at it—3.42.

'It's on the house,' he insisted when I asked him how much I owed him for the repair. He was adamant about it, so I thanked him profusely instead.

Before I left the shop, I turned to ask him:

'Uncle, what is the name of your late daughter?'

'Oh.' He pointed at the board outside. 'It's the name on the board.'

'Nini,' I muttered under my breath.

◆

On the walk back, I had a why-not moment and jumped into one of the cafés for a cup of coffee. As I waited for my order, I let my mind wander to a not-so-distant memory when I was in a similar café, with my sick father seated across the table. I can vividly recall what he had that day: ginger tea with a slice of cheese quiche, which he only had a mouthful of.

'Don't blame your mother,' he told me just as we got up to leave.

While waiting an eternity for my order, I replayed those words over and over in my mind, and the story of the uncle and his daughter, until something clicked inside me.

When my order was laid out on the table by the waiter, I reached into my pocket and pulled out the phone. After a moment of staring at the blank screen, I switched it on, scrolled through my contacts to get to a particular name, and pressed call.

Time

'Hello, Okharo,' said the voice on the other end.

'How are you, Mom?' It was the first time we were speaking in four years.

Scared Crow

'How long has it been anyway?'

I gathered my body into a steady mass, embracing all of my being. The fully-packed Tata Sumo taxi lurched forward through serpentine roads, zipping through an ever-passing landscape of sal, deodar and dust-bathed shrubs, with intermittent sightings of empty, half-walled resting sheds. In some of those sheds, scrawny women with paan-stained teeth sat idly, waiting for a surprise sale to conclude the day's slow business.

The question had two answers.

The first answer: It had been four wretched hours since I, squeezed into the backseat of a Tata Sumo, had been questioning my misplaced doggedness to make it to my native village, Chudi, whatever the discomfort along the way. I was, as I would like tell others, on a noble mission of academia.

In those four hours or so, filled with gut-churning turns and nauseating jerks, I took stock of my fellow passengers, and by the time the taxi came to halt at a shabby roadside hotel in Sanis for a quick tea break, I started to believe that I had forged a certain kinship with all of them—the single-serving kind, like the paper cups in the roadside hotel.

On the front seat, there sat two ladies who couldn't stop gossiping about a certain Lily whom they both hated with concerted passion. In the middle seat a father-and-son duo, who didn't talk much but would ask the driver to stop every now and then to take a leak, much to the exasperation of everyone. Beside them were three adolescents, dressed in knock-off streetwear and clearly drunk on some cheap, foul-smelling liquor. They spoke in a profanity-laced lingo that made no sense to me, or even perhaps to them. In the backseat, there was a couple who made their affection for each other known to all of us by blasting Bryan Adams's hits on their phones on loop, and then there was this gaon bura with a waggish moustache who embarked on a self-appointed mission to ceaselessly lecture his co-passengers about the vile obscenity of miniskirts and jeans and how it was gnawing away at the fabric of our glorious society.

The second answer: It has been seventeen years since my last visit.

Seventeen years ago, I came to my native village, Chudi, as a clueless town kid who didn't do much around the village but chase the wind with his gimcrack newspaper kite. It had been the village's golden jubilee celebration.

Being a town kid who was visiting the village for the first time had its perks, the most obvious being the endless dinner invitations from relatives near and distant. I was

A Kite of Farewells

literally hopping from one kitchen to another, being fed with everything from pig fat to roasted squirrels. It took me some time to get used to the raja machis, a necessary addition in every meal.

◆

'I can't drive any further. All of you should get off here. The junction is just over there,' the driver hurriedly shouted from the steering wheel.

My immediate reaction to that statement was regret at not informing my cousin beforehand to come and pick me up. The expensive cost of that omission—hauling my luggage up the steep steps to reach the village.

Thud. Thud. The driver tossed the luggage from the roof of the taxi without an iota of concern, but the marked look of exhaustion in his face made this callous display of shot-put with our luggage a tad excusable. After the last piece of luggage hit the ground, he let out a loud yawn to announce that he was clocking out. A thought raced through my head about what I, Renthungo, a five-feet-six-inch-tall excuse of a man, would do in a hypothetical scenario where my luggage was damaged from the impact and I would have to confront the driver, who was built like a tank. Thankfully, it remained just a thought.

Welcome to Chudi Village.
ESTD: 1932.
The village gate proclaimed overhead.

As I made my way up the steps hauling my luggage in wobbly jerks, I rummaged through my mind to try to remember the face of my cousin whom I had not seen in ages. Aremo was his name.

'I hope Aremo still remembers me,' I prayed.

The last time we saw each other was five years ago when he had accompanied Atsu on her monthly visit to the town. He had met with an accident and walked with a limp. Although he didn't speak much, he was amiable and always on call to attend to Atsu's needs.

'Aremo is the best son I never had,' Atsu would often quip.

As indispensable as he was in keeping the old house running, there was also another reason why Atsu kept him around: his parents had passed away, leaving him, a child of five then, at the mercy of a life in the village whose population was growing thin with each passing year, as most of the people moved en masse to the town following the allure of a better life.

'Oh Ren,' Aremo called from the kitchen door on seeing me at the gate drenched in sweat. 'You should have told me to come and pick you at the junction.'

Well, I do remember that amiable face now.

♦

The next morning, I woke up to the sight of Aremo holding a tray with a steaming cup of tea and some kata biskot dangerously close to my face. Judging by the unopened

A Kite of Farewells

suitcases huddled in a corner of the room, I might have headed straight to bed yesterday after a quick wash. I graciously accepted the tea and proceeded to dunk the kata biskot in it, a childhood habit that has stuck through adulthood.

Later, I went looking around the house; it had held its own against the ravages of time for the last sixty years, as a sturdy keeper of memories of all the people who had occupied its hallowed space.

The majhung hung lazily over the garden, now dense with sturdy pines, laden mango trees, and dark, luxuriant bushes. The joka didn't look that different from last time, but the utensils got a modern upgrade to the shiny stainless-steel ones. The garish green door sported a fresh coat of paint; the cretonne curtains stirring in the calm breeze looked immaculate; the white-washed, wooden bargeboard stood out the most, cutting a dominating figure from a height, though the buffalo skull nailed to the gable looked like an unnecessary indulgence.

The only apparent change was the neighbours, whose faces all looked new and young, and the conspicuous horde of crows that would noisily swoop down onto the tin roof and disappear into the ceiling through the vent. There was something about the crows that made me wrinkle my nose with morbid disgust.

After an exhaustive reconnaissance of the neighbourhood, I headed back to the joka to lunch on raja machi chutney and sticky rice.

With the heavy lunch settling down, I got out my itinerary and pored over it.

Interview elders who are an authority on 'Naga society before the advent of Christianity', read the first entry.

My train of thoughts chugged through the dimly lit stations of past events, with the loudest being the one with Professor Srinivas, a burnt-out professor of anthropology at St. Anthony, scoffing loudly at me in front of his colleagues and casting aspersions on the prospect of my thesis.

'I don't care what, and how you do it. I want it on the table by the month's end.'

The professor's croaky voice still rang in my ears.

The upside of this whole affair—doing independent research—was that it gave me a much-needed break from the petty schemes and scholarship politics of Professor Srinivas.

◆

Itinerary #1: Meet Amotsu Mhonlumo.
Amotsu Mhonlumo, one of the oldest men in the village, was the last of the dissident group who refused to embrace Christianity; he stuck with the old religion, which made him a persona non grata in the village. He was also believed to possess the ability to communicate with spirits in dreams, a topic which greatly interested me.

He lived in an old, thatched hut overlooking a garden of about two acres. I had already asked my resourceful cousin to make an appointment with him prior to my arrival and he didn't disappoint; he had already packed a gift of the

A Kite of Farewells

first harvest rice and vegetables from the garden for me to take along for Amotsu.

◆

The sun was at its peak, scorching the sporadic tin roofs that dotted this village nested in a verdant mountain with the bellowing Pofu running through the valley. In another six hours, the sun would disappear into the ridges of the Tiyi hills, and night would blanket this small village with its crescent pale moon and starry glitters. I made a mental note to return before dusk as the night would be pitch black owing to the routine load shedding that the electricity department had imposed on all the villages in the Lower Range.

◆

'Would you like a mouthful of zutsu before we start our interview?' Amotsu called out from the kitchen as I grabbed myself a moora to sit, rehearsing all the possible questions that I would be asking him in a minute.

The gifts from Aremo laid on the kitchen table had been opened and rigorously inspected by Amotsu, which I found a little weird.

I politely refused his offer of rice beer. Its pungent smell invaded every inch of the living space.

Amotsu poured a generous fill into his crude bamboo mug for himself and sat down on a moora facing me.

'Your grandparents were kind to me even when the entire village avoided me like a plague. For that, I am grateful to your family, and I am deeply sorry that your grandparents didn't live long enough to see all of you grow up to be fine men and women.'

I wondered how he would feel saying the same if he knew the state of things back at home, with a difficult brother possibly on the verge of alcohol addiction, and parents whose communication was limited to sneering at each other at the dinner table.

'How old are you, Amotsu?' I steered the course of our inchoate conversation towards my research work.

'If I remember right—' He took a mighty sip from his bamboo mug '—I believe I'm in the vicinity of grand old sixty-eight.'

The bottom of his mug peeked at me after two more questions, and by the time I had the satisfaction of asking him a dozen more, a smoky kerosene lamp went up by the door post, heralding the end of the day's business.

As I was making my way out the door, Amotsu called out to me, 'Tell your cousin the gift will be delivered tomorrow.' This confused me as I thought the gift of rice and vegetables sent by Aremo were meant for him alone. But I didn't want to burden him with more questions, so I nodded at him and hurried back home.

My walk back was faintly lit by the yellowish-orange glow of kerosene lamps, emanating from the few thatched houses straddling the kaccha road. It took considerable effort—hopping over water-logged potholes and other potential hazards in that scant lighting.

A Kite of Farewells

It would only be the day after when I would take a good look at the trousers from the previous pothole-hopping night against the morning light; I was both aghast and weirdly delighted by the artistic spattering of mud all over it. Aremo had a good laugh at my expense before he offered to wash it for me.

'This would require a special soap to wash it off,' he said between bouts of laughter. I politely refused his offer.

'Okay then, I will go into the kitchen and make us breakfast.'

When he disappeared into the kitchen, I remembered something I had been meaning to ask him.

'Aremo,' I called out. 'Remember the gift you sent me yesterday for Amotsu? Well, he said something about him delivering it tomorrow. Do you have any idea what he was talking about?'

'Oh, the gift? It's not for him.'

'For whom is it then?' I asked.

'It is for Atsu. I always send the first harvest to her. She is in Echu Li, you know,' he clarified.

I waited for the weight of his words to sink in, perhaps even expecting him to come out laughing from the kitchen telling me it's a joke.

All I heard from the kitchen was him asking, 'Do you want me to make anything specific?'

I decided not to pursue the conversation any further and blamed my confusion on the lack of context.

Sometime later, breakfast was served: an omelette with a

cup of black tea. We sat out under the morning sun peeking through the foliage in the garden.

When we got talking about the morning, the village, my work and more, I remembered another thing from the previous night that greatly bothered me—the crows.

'Did the crows in the ceiling wake you up last night?' I asked.

'Yes, more than once. I have tried everything to chase them away but they somehow find their way back to the ceiling every night.'

'There.' He pointed to the roof. 'Next to the dish antenna, there is a vent from where they enter. I had boarded the vent shut with plywood last month, but those headstrong rascals found their way inside even through that.'

I craned my neck up to catch a glimpse of the mentioned vent. The dish antenna blanketed in dust was all that I saw from the distance.

That night I was woken up at an ungodly hour by the swift sound of something heavy alighting on the tin roof, followed by heavy dragging of feet in the ceiling.

I turned on the phone's flashlight and pointed it at the ceiling to make sense of the activity coming from it.

I heard something heavy fall on the ground in Aremo's room, through the plywood wall that separated his room from mine, so I supposed he too was awakened by the sounds.

'Aremo, are you up? I called.

I pressed my ear against the plywood wall only to hear

A Kite of Farewells

the muffled sound of him talking, as if he was conversing with someone.

'Who could he be talking to at this hour?' I wondered.

I walked out of my room and knocked on his door. After some time, he popped his head out from the door, fully awake and beaming with joy.

'Did you hear something moving in the ceiling a while ago?' I asked sternly.

'I did not hear anything,' he replied.

'Okay, but I also heard you talking to someone. Do you have a guest over?' I continued.

'No, that was just Atsu,' he said bluntly.

'What?' I was at the cusp of shouting.

'She passed away three years ago. How do you—' I persisted.

But he promptly cut me off.

'Her spirit comes to visit me whenever I send her gifts in Echu Li. This is the third time this year.'

I was getting annoyed by the minute, and since it was late in the night, I didn't pursue the conversation any further. I hurried back to my room saving all the questions in my mind for the early morning.

Sleep did not come easy that night as I tossed and turned for hours trying to silence the barrage of questions multiplying inside my mind: what if Aremo is traumatized by Atsu's passing and fake-talking to her is his coping mechanism? What if he has gone full mental? But what if, by some miracle, he is indeed talking with the spirit of Atsu? Should I tell my folks about this?

I had no answers for any of the questions except the last one, which was a resounding no. Knowing my folks and their proclivity for believing anything hocus-pocus, they wouldn't hesitate to pull the plug on my research.

'Pack your bags and get on the first bus you see,' would be their unanimous call.

So like the rational man I pride myself to be, I decided to see through this. After all, it had more to do with Aremo than me, I reasoned.

◆

I waited out, sleepless and agitated, the longest night of my life, and as soon as I heard the kitchen door being swung open, I launched myself out of the bed.

'Hey Aremo, I got to ask you something about last night. Can you elaborate more about Atsu's visit?' The question startled him enough to toss away the lock in his hand.

From the furrows in my brow, he sensed my scepticism. 'I hope you don't think of me as crazy?'

'No, that's not what I meant.' The sound of a loud gulp escaped my mouth.

'Okay then, let me first get a fire going in the kitchen. Go wash up and come back. I promise I'll tell you everything.'

◆

'So, about Atsu's visit,' Aremo sighed as I looked at him with eager anticipation.

'It all started about a year and a half ago when I went

A Kite of Farewells

to Amotsu Mhonlumo with a gift for Atsu. I heard from one of the neighbours that in Amotsu's recent visit to Echu Li, he had seen Atsu looking vagrant.'

He looked into the far distance, sighed again, and continued.

'Atsu was like a mother to me, so upon hearing of Amotsu's Echu Li visit, I was saddened beyond words. I thought it would be in good faith if I sent something over to her; at least, that's what a dutiful son would do. The next night, the one after I had sent the gift to Amotsu, I had this strange dream. In the dream, Atsu told me that she would be coming to visit me in the living world. And visit she did.'

'How did the visit happen? In dreams?' I asked.

'No, it was not a dream,' he corrected. 'It's hard to describe the reality of it; it seems like a dream, yet it is not. In the first visit, Atsu was there in the flesh, but she looked different. Her face was pale and she wore a flowing black dress with jet-black feathers sticking to its seam. She also spoke in a hoarse voice.'

Sitting in silence, I tried hard to make sense of the story about Atsu's visit from Echu Li. I had too many questions and few answers.

I reckoned, after giving it due consideration, that it was best to pay Amotsu Mhonlumo a visit, though his explanation, like Aremo's story, might also require a suspension of disbelief. But that was the only way to get to the bottom of this.

◆

During breakfast, I mentally readied myself to navigate through the water-logged, pothole-ridden road to reach Amotsu's house, hopefully before he left for farm work.

When I got there, my shoes caked with mud, Amotsu was out in the garden plucking on the squash tendrils hanging from the bamboo trellises. Acknowledging my sudden visit, he dusted his army boots and ushered me into his kitchen. The kitchen under the morning light looked barer than the last time.

I did not waste much time in narrating what had transpired since my last visit. From the stoic expression on his face, I figured things like that were a common occurrence in his world. Or it may just be his age that had numbed him to the details of life. And just when I was regretting that I might have burdened him with my unannounced business, he exclaimed, 'Wait, did you say your Atsu was wearing a dress with black feathers?' He was taken aback. 'In my experience in Echu Li, people there don't wear black, and especially anything with feathers.'

I was at the frayed end of my wits. The air thick with tension was weighing down on my confused head.

'Amotsu, can you please explain everything in detail?' I asked.

'Ango, I know you townsfolk don't believe in Echu Li, but trust me when I tell you it's as real as this world is. It is not my duty to make a believer out of you today, but humour me for the first and last time, for what I am about to tell you is of paramount importance—it is a matter of

A Kite of Farewells

life and death.'

He composed himself on a moora and lit a biri. Speaking between quick puffs of his biri, his voice stern this time, he asked:

'Have you noticed any crows nesting in the house?'

'Y-yes...' I stuttered. 'How did you know?'

'That is a bad, bad omen.' A look of concern furrowed his brow. 'Echu Li is a world not different from ours. It is a transient stop for the dead before they move on to the Great Home, the final abode. They await their rewards in the Great Home, where they would become noble spirits, formless like the wind that winnows the grain and ageless like the stars. But while in Echu Li, they are forbidden to contact the living except in dreams.'

Notwithstanding my earlier scepticism, I found myself warming up to the idea—but not to the point of blunt acceptance—of Echu Li. I didn't want to derail the conversation by getting overtly critical as I felt the information Amotsu was giving me was important, whether I believed it or not.

So I asked:

'Aremo mentioned that you can visit Echu Li in your dreams. How does that work?'

'Ango, a dream is a portal into the unseen world, one beyond ours. I have inherited a special ability, like my father before me and my grandfather before him, that enables me to leave this mortal body and transcend into Echu Li in dreams, or through portals you now know them to be.'

He pulled me towards him.

'Now listen closely, I can go on and on about the specifics of Echu Li and more, but I'd be wasting both of our time. What I am about to tell you now is of grave importance to you and Aremo. It is something my grandfather told me on his deathbed; he whispered into my young ears that this special ability in our family is *a damned curse*, for it has a nefarious design. You see, not everyone in Echu Li was happy that the Great Father bestowed upon humans a chance to pass into the Great Home after they had served their time. This incensed a particular group of ancient spirits who felt that mortals shouldn't be allowed inside the Great Home. They rebelled against the Great Father and were swiftly defeated. As their punishment, the Great Father condemned them to wander the many subterranean worlds of Echu Li for all eternity. After aeons of aimless wandering, they came upon a plan to escape their tribulation. The key to their escape appeared one day when one of my ancestors, a living person, walked into Echu Li in his dream—a first by any human. They realized that the only way to escape their miserable existence was to escape from Echu Li altogether. To do so, they entrusted one among them to secretly tie a thread around my ancestor's foot. They hoped to follow the thread back to our world. This was necessary because the Great Father had once proclaimed that spirits from Echu Li would be lost in a labyrinth if they were to cross over to the living world. My grandfather told me that if they crossed over, they would latch onto the people sending gifts through the

A Kite of Farewells

person visiting Echu Li. He also told me that these spirits looked like crows.'

He walked over to his cupboard and started to rummage through its contents.

'Here.' He produced a jet-black feather. 'My grandfather handed me this just before he breathed his last.'

His voice became heavy. 'Some years after his passing, I heard from the village medicine man that his death was caused by the guilt of not being able to stop the many mysterious deaths of people in the village caused by a group of malevolent spirits that had followed him into our world during one of his visits to Echu Li. The medicine man mentioned a ritual my grandfather spoke of that could have prevented the deaths if he had done it on time.'

He stood up, took a deep breath and said:

'Now Ango, heed my words. A malevolent spirit has escaped from Echu Li and is now appearing to Aremo as your Atsu. If you want to live through this, do exactly what I am about to tell you. There will be a day when the malevolent spirit will reveal its true form. On that day, its heart will take the form of a crow. The crow will have jet-black feathers. You or Aremo are to kill that crow without hesitation and bury the feather inside your Atsu's coffin. The burial should be done before the end of the day after the act. Remember again—you should only kill the crow after the malevolent spirit reveals itself to you.'

With each word coming out Amotsu's mouth, things started to sound more and more outrageous. I stood still and listened, feeling the weight of the words sinking into my head.

'Malevolent spirits? Kill a crow? Bury the feather inside Atsu's coffin?' The words rang inside my head until something cold reached out from the darkness within and gripped me. Amotsu's words triggered a militant side of me that was foreign to me until then. I took a deep breath.

'Okay, I will do it,' I told Amotsu.

◆

Days passed but there was no sighting of the crow in question, or of the malevolent spirit in its true form. We even went up to the roof to check. During nights I laid on the bed, listening to the slow hum of the wind tearing from the bare frame of the roof. With nothing happening to cause supernatural alarm like Amotsu had mentioned, I threw myself into my research work that had been pending for some time.

I got busy courting the elders of the village, jotting whatever they said in my notebook as they regaled me with stories from the old days about the Great Wars, famines, myths and more. Some days I accompanied them to places of intimate association with their stories—decrepit morungs, old battlefields, lakes, caverns, and so on.

I was satisfied with this new state of living. I was learning more about the village and the people, and at the rate at which work was progressing, I opined that I might be wrapping up my research earlier than expected.

A Kite of Farewells

One night, after a tiring day of trekking to a nearby river and thereafter a scrumptious meal of mahseer fish cooked inside a bamboo culm, I drifted off to sleep. But an hour later, I was shaken awake by a bizarre dream.

I dreamt of Atsu. She appeared from the ceiling, hung upside down with a thick rope around her feet; she was crying out in distress. Behind her was Aremo, brandishing a bloodied knife and grinning devilishly at me. His eyes were black, devoid of life.

Shocked by the vivid visuals, I woke up nearly screaming. I quickly looked at my phone on the table: ten minutes past nine.

As my hand reached towards the switchboard, I heard peals of laughter grow in loudness and fill the whole house. The source of which was the room on the other side of the plywood wall—Aremo's room.

I bolted out of my room to Aremo's room, pushed the door open, then reached into the darkness of the room and flipped the light switch on.

In the seconds between darkness and the lights turning on, my eyes took notice of a large, feathery figure taking flight out of the open window, and morphing into a black crow when it met the air outside. In the middle of the room, sitting upright and facing the window was Aremo, with the same knife and rope from my dream. The cawing of the crow, now a fair distance away, echoed in the emptiness of the room along with the howling of the cold burst of wind through the window.

Scared Crow

'Aremo!'

I managed a panicky call after getting a grip on my senses, now amped up to eleven.

He sat still, unperturbed by my presence or whatever happened in the intervening moment. I registered a faint snigger from his mouth.

I cautiously walked towards him and gave him a gentle shake from behind—still no response. I turned him around and saw that his eyes were still closed like he was asleep. I thought for a moment, and then, with the calculated might of my right hand, I landed a quick slap on one of his cheeks to bring him to wakefulness.

He was not so pleased to be at the receiving end of such a brute method of summoning.

'Ren, what are you doing in my room? Why did you do that? And why am I holding these?' He tossed the knife and the rope away into the corner.

I made a speedy survey of the view outside the window in the hope that the sighting of the crow again would somehow answer all his questions. But it had disappeared like the way it appeared—like a mystery. I closed the window, shutting off whatever vestiges of mystery still lingered invisible to the eyes; and the godawful cold wind picked up in intensity.

Then for the next twenty minutes, I unpacked everything I had known and seen: Amotsu's warning, malevolent spirits, the spirit revealing its true form, appearance of the crow, and the dream from a while ago, as well as the shadowy figure that escaped out from the window.

A Kite of Farewells

Aremo listened keenly, nodding in agreement to everything except the last bit.

'It's Atsu. Trust me, it's her,' he pleaded.

'No, don't you see? It's the malevolent spirit Amotsu Mhonlumo warned me about,' I protested.

I tried again to persuade him, but it only made him more adamant.

Frustrated, I went out to get some air and zone out for a minute, away from this weird mess. Staring out into the night sky, I resolved that it was time my folks knew what was going on. I reached into the pocket of my jacket and got out my cell phone.

After the first few calls didn't connect due to poor network, I found myself racing up the shoddily cemented steps to the lone church. It was positioned conveniently on a hummock, with a commanding view of the whole village right down to the rotting palisades encircling the last house. I swung the phone in vain for some time hoping to get an extra bar, and when I managed to bring it to two bars, without a beat I pressed call.

'Hello, Ren?' said mom on the other end. 'Can you hear me?'

But the voice on the other end faded into irrelevance in the light of what caught my eye—a figure perched on the roof of the house, our house. Giving in to instincts, and against my better judgement, I pushed my person forward and squinted my eyes to the details of this frightening sight.

It turned its head towards me, sensing an unwelcome

observer. Although I couldn't put to words what greeted my eyes to a tenable description, two of its aspects stood out: its silhouette, human-like yet otherworldly, tapered into a thick plumage like that of a raven; and its eyes, glowing like the fiery coals of Baghty. I felt the hairs on my arms stand up.

In the gaze of its blazing eyes, a mysterious affliction came over me like ocean currents. I felt its gaze unravel my deepest and darkest secrets, leaving me naked and exposed. Then I was sucked into a trance, where I witnessed my entire life, from cradle to grave, in one quick succession. I stretched my hand out to grasp the moments slipping through my hand like sand. My head was about to explode from the onslaught of stimuli assaulting my senses. Then like a veil slipping off me, everything went silent and I came back to my senses.

Beep! The call disconnected.

I composed myself and looked at my phone.

When I moved my gaze to the roof, the figure had vanished into the dark night. A familiar voice started to stir inside my head, and slowly settled on my ears:

'Kill that crow without hesitation and bury the feather inside your Atsu's coffin...before the end of the day after the act.'

Amotsu's warning.

I walked back to the house still making sense of the true form of the malevolent spirit that Amotsu spoke of.

At the door, his figure silhouetted by the light from his room, Aremo was waiting with a crow and a bloodied knife in his hands.

A Kite of Farewells

'Hey Ren! Look, it's the crow you told me about. I killed it. It's over!' He waved the dead crow at me.

With a single deft stab to the heart, he had killed the crow. He explained:

'After you left suddenly, I went up to the roof to investigate the sound coming from it and found this crow nesting in a heap of rags. I got the rope from earlier, snuck up to it and lassoed it. Then hanging it upside down, I stabbed it till it stopped moving.'

'…bury the feather inside your Atsu's coffin…before the end of the day after the act,' Amotsu's words rang in my mind again. I reached for the dead crow and yanked a feather off it. It was black as the night. Then I looked at Aremo and instructed him to bury the crow in the garden.

I did not mention to him the figure on the roof. My focus zeroed in on the task at hand: I have to bury the feather inside Atsu's coffin by the end of next day. In other words, I had to dig up Atsu's coffin.

Sleep came easy that night as I dozed off the moment my body hit the bed. Early in the morning, much earlier than usual, I was woken up by the beating of log drums over warbling war cries. The sun wasn't even up yet. It sounded ominous.

I tried burying my head under the pillow to fight the noise, but it didn't help. So I got up reluctantly to find out the reason behind the early morning commotion.

Aremo, bent over the gate, was lighting incense sticks wedged into bamboo poles.

'What's this early morning ruckus all about?' I asked.

'Today is the day we commemorate the passing of the dead from Echu Li to the Great Home. This is one of the few practices from the olden days still observed by the whole village with reverence. It is advised that all the villagers abstain from hard labour the whole day.'

Without a single word more, I slipped into the kitchen and put together a hurried breakfast for myself. After an oily omelette and a cup of black tea, I asked Aremo for the directions to the village cemetery.

'It might rain. Take an umbrella,' Aremo cautioned from the gate. I was in a terrible hurry, so I didn't bother to run back to the house to get an umbrella. Besides, the weather seemed fine.

◆

The cemetery was located at the foot of the mountain, behind an unoccupied log cabin. Stones jutting out intermittently as markers straddled a dusty path stamped flat over weeds. It had all the unassuming characteristics of a graveyard except for the uncanny silence expected from a place like this; its south end terminated at a gorge, and the murmur of the rapids rose up and filled the cemetery.

Inside the log cabin, I found a dusty hammer and a shovel. The cabin was bare except for an old chair and a table.

Finding Atsu's grave wasn't hard; it was a modest one with a granite tombstone weathered around the edges and a wreath of greyed flowers rested against it.

A Kite of Farewells

I stood towering over the grave and whispered an apology. Then I started swinging the hammer on the cemented base of the grave. With each blow, the sound of the hammer coming down heavily on the hard surface rang through the cemetery and rose up the mountain.

Soon the soil under the base peeked through the rubble and I got out the shovel to dig into the soil. I was drenched in sweat.

When I kicked the shovel into the soil with the might of my whole body, the grey clouds gathering above roared to life as bolts of lightning ripped through the sky: rain was imminent.

I cursed at myself for not listening to Aremo earlier. The rain was going to make my commute up to the village a laborious one, as the only road from the cemetery was a kaccha one. I expeditiously picked up the pace of shovelling until a pile of soil stood atop the rubble beside the grave.

When my legs, now knee deep in the soil, started to exert from the labour, the expected happened—fine beats of drizzle slipped down my face, and soon I was fighting to keep my eyes open as it started to rain in torrents.

The only upside to the whole situation was that the soil, now softened by the rain, took less effort to dig.

With the rain growing in intensity, I persisted until my ears heard the most divine sound—the sound of the shovel hitting the coffin. I was elated at the discovery as my arms were getting sore.

I jammed the shovel into one of the sides of the coffin,

which, oddly, was in pristine condition. With all the strength I could summon, I pried the coffin open. The lid of the coffin came off with splinters flying into the air, to reveal its content—it was empty.

There was nothing inside, not even an outline in the white sheet laid inside it. It looked like it had been buried empty.

After the feeling of shock wore off, I unhesitatingly reached into the pocket of my jacket, got out the feather of the crow from last night, and tossed it into the empty coffin. 'I have to complete what Amotsu told me to do, regardless of the empty coffin,' I thought aloud. I had plenty of time to think about the absurdity of it on my way back.

I hurriedly shovelled the soil back atop the coffin and started to make my way up to the village. The way up was through a dense forest, up the muddy kaccha road.

A parting glance at the cemetery before I disappeared into the forest, and I was met with the regretful sight of the mess I had left behind: the sacredness of the cemetery defiled by my own hands.

With the rain pouring down on me as divine retribution, I pushed forward up to the village.

♦

Back in the village, the rain had taken a more menacing form as it bashed the corrugated roofs at regular intervals, its icy sheet tossed around by the squalling wind ripping through the empty footpath.

A Kite of Farewells

I did not see a single soul around except for a boy in a yellow raincoat on the balcony of a two-storeyed house, reaching his hand out from the railing.

I waved at the boy but he didn't notice me.

When I got back to my room, drenched from head to toe and my teeth chattering, I felt a searing pain in my chest. But thoroughly exhausted and wet as wet could be, I didn't bother to give it much thought. I got out of my wet clothes, tossed them into a corner, slipped into warm ones, and hit the sack. Sleep came without any struggle.

◆

Later, I woke up with a throbbing headache and a strange buzzing in my ears. The buzzing in my ears had pushed all of my senses to their edge, just a nudge away from insanity. My head felt heavy and my throat dry.

I got up from the bed and the buzzing grew louder, like the sound of a swarm of locusts so immense that it could black out the sky with its descent.

I parted the curtains and looked out the window: the sky looked unusual. It looked like a sea of blood. I was overcome with a feeling of intense loneliness, the likes of which I had never felt before.

'Aremo,' I shouted from the room but got no response.

With no signs of Aremo around the house, I got my phone out and frantically scrolled through the contacts. I held the phone to my ears, still buzzing, and waited for the call to get through.

Scared Crow

'Hello, Ren...' the voice on the other end of the phone put up a faint struggle and then went silent. I cursed at the network again.

I raced up the steps to the church. After some effort, I got the network reception up to two bars.

'Hello, Ren, I can't hear y-' The call dropped.

Beep! The network went cold.

'Ango Ren,' a familiar voice called out to me from the steps.

Amotsu Mhonlumo, with an olive haversack slung over his shoulder, waved at me.

'Stay right there. I have something for you,' he shouted from the distance.

Huffing and puffing, he made his way up the steps, and when I was within his arm's reach, he reached into his haversack and produced a plastic bag with rice and some bananas inside.

'Amotsu, what is this?' I asked, confused at the gesture.

'Ango, I came to bring you this gift from your cousin, Aremo,' he replied.

'I don't understand.' I made no effort in masking my annoyance.

'You don't know yet?' He sighed.

He gently placed his hand on my shoulder.

'Ango, remember the day you went to bury the feather, the day of the passing of the dead from Echu Li to the Great Home? You never came back. The next day, the whole village organized a search party to find you but to no avail; it was

A Kite of Farewells

only in the late evening when your cousin suggested that we look for you at the cemetery that we found you—your body—curled up inside a coffin, grasping a black feather. There were no bruises on your body to suggest any signs of struggle. When the doctor from the next village arrived late at night—his distinct yellow raincoat announcing his arrival from a distance—he confirmed that you had suffered a fatal heart attack.'

'Tell me you are joking, Amotsu!' I exclaimed.

Out of the corner of my eye, I noticed something odd about the sky besides its uncanny hue—there were two suns in the sky.

'But Amotsu, I was on the phone with my mom just a while ago,' I argued.

'Well, was she able to hear you?' Amotsu asked.

'No, but—' On the verge of tears, I stuttered, 'T-the network was... I just want to go h-home.'

Amotsu looked at me, his eyes full of pity.

'Ango,' he paused, 'this is now your home—this is Echu Li.'

The Newspaper Kite

THERE ARE LEVELS TO THE sky that only a kite pieced together from an old newspaper can soar to—levels unreached by any other kite regardless of its clever design or the deft hands delicately guiding its ascent.

A rowdy group of four brothers pulled at their extra-large newspaper kite, wonky in motion, in large part due to its poor construct, shouting at the top of their lungs as if it was more than just the wind that was aiding its crooked ascension.

'Pull left,' shouted Ben, the eldest, as he towered over his brothers, his hands cupped like a binocular to his squinted eyes. This was the second kite to take flight that day, the first having been a sad disappointment, lifting off the ground after much running only to flop down in a zigzag path into the neighbour's garden. The owner of the garden, a lady in her late fifties, had a reputation of throwing fiery temper tantrums over the silliest of matters. Last month, she kept shouting for hours without a quiver in her tone when one

A Kite of Farewells

of the boys scooped a sixer into the garden during their weekend cricket match with the other colony boys.

It was a magnificent hit, and the boys roared in excitement when the ball took its trajectory, peaking mid-flight some two feet above the roof only to hastily descend, to loud gasps, into the fenced garden. The moment the ball hit the ground, the lady craned her neck from the kitchen, her eyes like circling vultures and her mouth foaming with abuses of the vilest kind. The boys quickly dispersed from the area, stealing from it all signs of life and excitement. The vicinity was swept with the loud shouting of the lady, which went on for hours. Even the crickets took leave of their choral routine, and the birds disappeared from the sky above.

◆

Later that evening, after the kite fiasco, there was a knock on the door of the boys' house—a stone's throw away from the lady's. While the boys opened the door expecting to see the lady, there stood her husband—a gentleman in his mid-sixties whose demeanour was starkly different from his wife's. They also looked different: the lady had a face that just refused to be easy on the eyes, whereas her husband looked kind and had a warm smile. The boys lovingly called him Amotsu.

Amotsu, standing at the door, pulled out the kite that had zipped into their garden.

'Boys, I think this is yours.' He handed them the kite. 'I have made some repairs to it.'

The kite now sported a new frame and a flowing paper tail.

The Newspaper Kite

'Let's fly this kite tomorrow,' Ben exclaimed to loud cheers from his brothers. Amotsu nodded in approval.

The next day, Amotsu and the boys walked up the colony's rugged steps, shoddily built from rough-cut boulders, and reached the colony junction. The road around the junction wore a new coat of black topping. There were talks around the colony that the black topping was good till the monsoon arrived and washed it all away.

The colony kids, in the spirit of true pragmatism, took full advantage of the supposed short-lived convenience of the black topping by getting on their bicycles and whatever had wheels on it, to do laps of merry riding till their parents came searching for them with a stick in hand. The adults sulked at the new-found cacophonous pastime of the kids.

'Amotsu, pull to the left!' The boys watched in awe as Amotsu masterfully guided the kite over the corrugated sheet-roofs of government quarters. Their kite, though exhibiting a convincing tenacity that day, snapped abruptly and drifted away with the wind blowing from the east.

The wind soon grew in strength and grey clouds gathered above. The once-tranquil expanse was now a stage for the rumbling symphony of an impending storm. This natural orchestra, with its low and resonant thunder, rose to a crescendo and resolved into a staccato of droplets descending on the boys and Amotsu. Before they could get stuck in the storm, they scurried back to their homes.

Back at home, with the sky starting to clear a bit, the boys watched from the grilled window—their hands stretched out,

A Kite of Farewells

trying to catch the raindrops slipping down the corrugated tin roof—the wobbly voyage of a paper boat they had made by folding a sheet of paper. The paper boat rocked from side to side in the foot-sized drain, and eventually disappeared around the corner where the drain met a larger drain.

'We should give our next boat a special name.'

One of the boys got out an ink pen from his school bag and proceeded to write 'Shaktimaan' in cursive. The other boys applauded at his ingenuity. Lofty ideas are, to an extent, a luxury when the means to materialize it are limited or absent. When you are poor, you train your mind to dream on a budget, and some days, you surprise yourself by getting so much out of so little.

The paper boat with 'Shaktimaan' written on its hull did much better than its predecessor; it kept intact its shape as the water in the drain threw it against the sides, rocking it at angles, leading to the name being smudged to appear like a Rorschach ink blot.

◆

As the night fell slowly and then all at once, mellow tunes from an old radio hummed against the monotonic chirping of the crickets in the background. Amotsu had this habit of welcoming the night with the radio beside him, his one arm hanging from the window of the sitting room, dreamily looking out at the night sky. He said that under the blanket of the night, everything with a name became one. The flowers blowing in the wind were no different from the rocks rolling

The Newspaper Kite

down the ravine; everything—the beautiful and the bland—assumed a look of sameness. The only thing that stood out were the stars, shining above like a celestial net cast over the bare bosom of the night.

That night's special was the hits of Perry Como. The boys rushed to the window of the common room to listen to the crooner on the radio. Amotsu, upon seeing the boys at the window, would turn up the volume and place the radio down on the windowsill, facing the boys. The radio was usually placed on a three-legged stool under the window.

◆

'Don't enter,' screeched the lady from the kitchen door as Ben approached. There was an obvious look of anger on her face at his intrusion; only this time, he wasn't intruding. He had been sent by his mother with a plate of pork innards for the lady.

Ben failed to understand the cordial relationship between the lady and his mother, which in the past few months had become even warmer. He supposed that the lady being childless and Mother still recovering from the death of her mother a year ago had something to do with it.

Last month, when the lady had returned from Kohima, she brought a red shawl for Mother—she hadn't bought anything for her husband or herself. Her face beamed with joy for the first time that year when mother wore that shawl to church.

'Mother sent this.' Ben produced the plate from the door. The lady promptly snatched the plate from Ben and laid it

A Kite of Farewells

down on the stool for her beady-eyed guests, who, through the cigarette-smoke plume, looked at him in unison.

Each one of them had in their hands a pannikin cup full of the foul-smelling local liquor, zutsu. They swigged it in loud gulps, letting out an occasional self-congratulatory 'aghh' as if they were drinking the elixir of gods. As he waited at the door for the lady to return the plate, one of the guests remarked something while pointing in his direction, which made Ben very conscious.

◆

The boys huddled around their father as he prised open the plastic bag in his hand revealing its sorry content of second-hand treasures: boarding school tees in faded colours, dog-eared activity books, chewed out stationery items, and a bunch of hard-boiled candy with fancy wrappers the likes of which the boys had never seen until that day.

The well-off cousins residing in the next colony had returned from their boarding schools for vacation and were relinquishing their old uniforms and used belongings. On many occasions, the spoilt cousins would openly deny any relation to the boys when they were spotted together by their equally privileged peers.

This timely generosity of hand-me-downs from the cousins was the only thing that made the boys believe that they were related.

That night, as each of the boys lay on the single shared bed, with an extra-large mink blanket over them and their

The Newspaper Kite

'new' possessions in hand, their minds drifted off into the inviting open pastures of tomorrow and the many wonderful things they could do with their new belongings.

The fantastical imagination of childhood sweetens even the pain of a life lived on the bare minimum.

◆

The boys had never seen Father so angry, even though when under the influence of alcohol he was known to be quite unreasonable. That day, the first Saturday of December, Father dragged his inebriated self into their Christmas camp put together with tarpaulin sheets and bamboo sticks, his speech slurring, his gait ungainly, and then, without any provocation or reason, proceeded to kick at the tarpaulin walls.

The boys and their friends, who were bartering stories around a small bonfire when Father barged in, watched in silent bewilderment as their Christmas fantasy was stamped to smithereens by a drunken manchild. With their Christmas camp now turned to broken sticks and torn tarpaulin sheets, December offered little joy to the boys.

The next day, Father redeemed himself by gathering the boys at the dining table and gifting them new crayons sets to draw their dream houses; A4 paper sheets with garish colours and crude geometry of shaky lines resembling in some parts stairs, windows and balconies were tacked to the mud-plastered wall of the kitchen for the doting eyes of the boys for the next two weeks.

◆

A Kite of Farewells

With December slipping off like a thief in the night, the year came to an end just like that. The new year, after the expected frenzy of New Year's Eve, also settled in quietly like the dust on the once-black-topped road around the junction.

One listless February evening, the stillness in the air, typical of that month of the year, was shaken to activity—the boys looked out of the window of the common room to find a growing congregation of colony folks outside the house next door—Amotsu's house.

A loud cry shot through the growing murmur of the crowd outside the house. It was obvious—a sudden demise. And judging by the distinct shrill cry of the lady, Amotsu was no more. He had passed away in his sleep, his beloved radio playing by his side.

◆

When they lowered his coffin into the grave, the boys standing behind their mother wept conspicuously, and upon the insistence of mother, took turns to say farewell to Amotsu.

'There is always a next day,' Amotsu would often say to them, but even with their naive understanding of life, they knew that the next day would be a day without Amotsu.

There was a certain air of indignation around his sudden demise, but equally there was also a feeling of gratitude for the life of Amotsu, whom everyone remembered as a generous and loving man. The people around spoke of how, on many occasions, he had gone out of his way to help them.

◆

The Newspaper Kite

'Pull a little to the left. No, to the right!' The boys directed Ben as he struggled with the newspaper kite now sporting a sturdier frame—something they came up with after improving on the previous designs.

'Hold steady!' An excited shout rang out.

The wind swooped in and lifted the kite up, throwing the paper strips glued to its tail into a fluttery dance. In its ascent, it looked like a bird that had broken free from its cage.

'Remember that thread trick Amotsu used to do?' The boys called out to Ben.

Ben pulled at the thread with pronounced effort at calculated intervals—Amotsu's trick. The wind was picking up in speed, aiding the kite's ascent. But a little mistake could end it all—the kite was at a height where the thread was usually known to give away. The kite still held, rising gradually with the wind.

'This is a new record!' the boys cheered.

There are levels to the sky that only a kite pieced together from a newspaper can soar to. That day, under the heat of the swelling afternoon sun, a symbol of defiance, a newspaper kite, belonging to four rowdy boys, soared to a realm where dreams, however lofty, are made real.

A miracle for something so poorly made.

Acknowledgements

I would like to express my heartfelt gratitude to many individuals who have contributed to the creation of this book.

Avinuo Kire, you inspired courage in the hearts of young Naga writers like me through your fearless writings. Your mentorship has been indispensable and critique valuable.

Mhaya, I am grateful to you for believing in this book when it was just wispy ideas floating in the air.

The meticulous editing, insightful feedback, and commitment to improving the manuscript of my editor Smita Mathur are also appreciated.

Family and friends, thank you for your encouragement, support, and understanding during this journey. Without your collective efforts, this book would not have been possible. Thank you for being part of this adventure!

www.ingramcontent.com/pod-product-compliance
Lightning Source LLC
Chambersburg PA
CBHW030219170426
43194CB00007BA/799